EASA STUDY GUIDES

MASS & BALANCE

MASS & BALANCE

Dr. Stuart E. Smith

STUDY GUIDE SERIES for EASA examinations

Copyright of this publication remains with the author Dr. Stuart E. Smith. The right of Dr. Stuart E. Smith to be identified as author of this publication has been asserted in accordance with the Copyright, Designs and Patents Act, 1988. You are not permitted to sell, loan or otherwise make this publication available to another person. No part of this publication may be copied, reproduced, translated, or reduced to any electronic medium or machine-readable form without the prior written consent of Dr. Stuart E. Smith. ©2002-2009. All rights reserved.

In no event shall Dr. Stuart E. Smith be liable for any damages whatsoever (including without limitation damages for loss of business profits, business interruption, or other pecuniary losses) arising out of the use of or inability to comprehend this publication.

British Library Cataloguing in Publication Data.
A catalogue record for this book is pending from the British Library.

First published in the United Kingdom by Cranfield Aviation Training School Limited. 2002

Further volumes in this series are:
Aircraft General Knowledge: Airframes / Systems / Electrics / Powerplant / Emergency Equipment
Air Law
Flight Planning & Monitoring
General Navigation
Human Performance
Instrumentation
Meteorology
Operational Procedures
Performance
Principles of Flight
Radio Navigation
VFR & IFR Communications

Series editor: Dr. Stuart E. Smith

 **CRANFIELD AVIATION TRAINING SCHOOL LTD. PART-FCL ATO N° 276**
CATS INNOVATION CENTRE, LUTON, Bedfordshire LU2 8DL U.K.

www.catsaviation.com

EASA STUDY GUIDES

MASS & BALANCE

CHAPTER 1	Introduction to Mass and Balance	1-1
1.1	Introduction	1-2
CHAPTER 2	Centre of Gravity	2-1
2.1	Determination of CG	2-3
2.1.1	Definitions	2-3
CHAPTER 3	STABILITY	3-6
3.1	Definition: Static and Dynamic Stability	3-6
3.1.1	Static stability	3-6
3.1.2	Dynamic stability	3-7
3.1.3	Centre of gravity and centre of pressure	3-9
3.1.4	Moment and stability of the isolated wing	3-10
3.1.5	Moment and stability of the entire aircraft	3-12
3.2	Longitudinal Stability	3-13
3.2.1	Definition of the tailplane as main stabilising factor	3-13
3.2.2	Neutral point	3-16
CHAPTER 4	Static Margin and MAC	4-1
4.1.1	Mean Aerodynamic Chord (MAC)	4-1
4.1.2	Example 1	4-2
4.2	Practical calculations to Determine CG	4-4
4.2.1	Example 1	4-4
4.3	Centre of Gravity of an Aeroplane	4-5
4.4	Fuel Calculations	4-6
4.4.1	To convert USG into lbs	4-6
4.4.2	Calculations with Specific gravity	4-6
4.5	Moving the Centre of Gravity	4-7
4.5.1	Example 1	4-7
4.5.2	Example 1	4-8
4.6	Adding or Removing a Weight	4-9
4.6.1	Example 1	4-9
CHAPTER 5	Practical Methods of Calculating Payload	5-1
5.1	Useful load	5-3
5.2	Using the Load and Trim Sheet	5-5
CHAPTER 6		6-1
Floor Loading		6-1
6.1	Distribution Load:	6-1
6.2	Running Load:	6-2
CHAPTER 7		7-1
Loading a Single-Engine Piston Aeroplane		7-1
7.1	Introduction	7-1
7.1.1	Example 1	7-1
7.1.2	Example 2	7-3
CHAPTER 8	Loading a Light Twin-Engine Piston Aeroplane	8-1
8.1	Introduction	8-1
8.1.1	Example 1	8-1
CHAPTER 9	Loading a Transport Aeroplane	9-1
9.1	Introduction	9-1
9.1.1	Use of Passenger Mass, Crew Mass Data	9-6
9.1.1.1	Example 1	9-6

CRANFIELD AVIATION TRAINING SCHOOL LTD. PART-FCL ATO N° 276
CATS INNOVATION CENTRE, LUTON, Bedfordshire LU2 8DL U.K.

www.catsaviation.com

EASA STUDY GUIDES

MASS & BALANCE

CHAPTER 1
Introduction to Mass and Balance

JAR-FCL REF NO LEARNING OBJECTIVES
031 00 00 00 MASS AND BALANCE
031 03 00 00 CENTRE OF GRAVITY (C.G)

031 03 01 00 Basis of C.G. Calculations

031 03 01 01 Datum
Explain the term datum.
Find the datum position from an aeroplane-operating manual for calculation purposes.

031 03 01 02 Moment arm
Explain the moment arm and its algebraic sign.
Extract moment arms for different loading positions from aeroplane operating manual

031 03 01 03 Moment
Explain the term "moment" and calculate examples.
Explain the term "index" and interpret an example of an index formula.
Calculate the index with given weight, centre of gravity and index formula and vice versa

031 03 01 04 Expression in percentage of mean aerodynamic chord (% MAC)
Explain the general equation for the centre of gravity.
Illustrate the advantage of using % MAC as an expression for the centre of gravity location.
Calculate centre of gravity positions and express them in % MAC

031 03 02 00 Calculation of C.G.
031 03 02 01 Centre of gravity at empty mass
Calculate the aeroplane centre of gravity from scale readings at weighing.
Find the centre of gravity at the dry operating mass from the aeroplane manual.

031 03 02 02 Movement of C.G with addition of fuel, load and ballast
Calculate the effect of shifting loads or additional loads on the centre of gravity.
Describe the influence of fuel loading or usage on the centre of gravity.
Extract the data for the influence of fuel on the centre of gravity from an aeroplane operating manual.

031 03 02 03 Practical methods of calculation
Calculate zero fuel, takeoff and landing masses, the respective moments and centre of gravity positions with the aid of various types of mass and balance documentations
Mass and balance documents of various aircraft types
Explain the differences between operational and certified limits for the centre of gravity.
State where the certified and where the operational limits can be found and extract them

031 03 03 00 Securing of Load
031 03 03 01 Importance of adequate tie-down
Describe the reasons why loads in cabin and cargo rooms have to be secured or tied down.
State that cargo aeroplanes use pallets or containers to secure the load

031 03 03 02 Effect of loadshift
Effect of Loadshift See 031 03 02 02

031 03 04 00 Area Load, Running Load, Supporting See 031 01 02 02

CRANFIELD AVIATION TRAINING SCHOOL LTD. PART-FCL ATO N° 276
CATS INNOVATION CENTRE, LUTON, Bedfordshire LU2 8DL U.K.

www.catsaviation.com

EASA STUDY GUIDES

MASS & BALANCE

1.1 Introduction

The subject Mass and Balance is concerned with ensuring that, when an aeroplane is dispatched, it is not overloaded nor incorrectly loaded. Overloading and incorrect loading both lead at the very least to inefficient operation and at the worst to a dangerous flying condition. The aeroplane commander is responsible for ensuring that the aeroplane is correctly loaded. Someone else may well have worked out the detail, but, as with many other aspects of aeroplane operation, the ultimate responsibility is with the aircraft commander. It is therefore critically important that the potential commander not only understands the problem, but is also able to demonstrate his competence to the examining authority.

> The Commander has ultimate responsibility for the loading of the aircraft

There are three classes of aircraft to be studied:
- A single engine piston not certified under JAR25 (Light Aeroplanes) Performance Class B (SEP1)
- A multi engine piston not certified under JAR25 (Light Aeroplanes) Performance Class B (MEP1)
- A medium range twin jet certified under JAR25 Performance Class A (MRJT)

A set of data sheets has been published for use in the European Professional Pilots Licence Examinations for Mass and Balance. The data sheets cover the three classes of aeroplane and are printed under the title CAP 696 which must be obtained for your study.

Compliments of Flight International

Figure 1.1 Neglecting mass and balance

CHAPTER 2
Centre of Gravity

The centre of gravity of a body is that point through which the sum of the forces of all masses of the body is considered to act and is situated on the longitudinal axis, acting parallel to the gravity vector both in the air and on the ground

In level flight, mass acting through the centre of gravity (CG) is balanced by lift acting through the centre of pressure (CP). The Centre of Lift (C of L) rarely coincides with the Centre of Gravity (CG). During flight both the C of P and CG move. The CG moves due to passenger movement and the consumption of fuel.

Any discrepancy between CG and C of L causes a pitching moment:

- If the CG is forward of the C of L there is a nose heavy moment

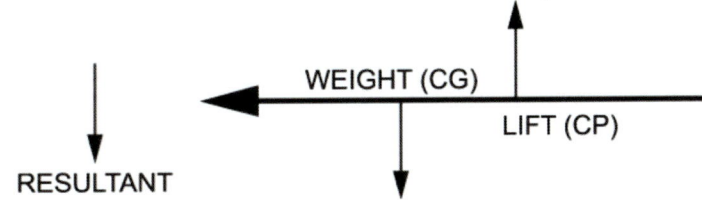

Figure 2.1 Nose Heavy

- If the CG is aft of C of L there is a tail heavy moment.

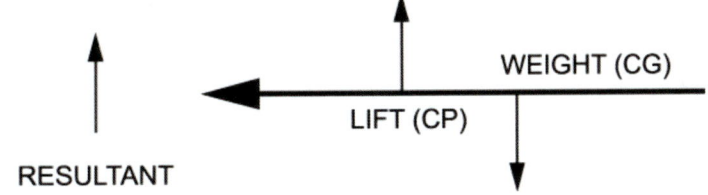

Figure 2.2 Tail Heavy

Such pitching moments are counteracted by moving the elevator to maintain level flight. This is normally achieved by trimming the elevator. Any such trimming may result in an increase in profile drag, reducing efficiency and range, because of higher fuel consumption to overcome the additional drag by increasing the power setting. If the CG range is large, elevator trimming could result in reduced pitch control. The following table shows the effects of a forward or aft CG on various flight characteristics:

	CG at Forward Limit	**CG at Aft limit**
Pitch	Stable	Unstable
Stalling Speed	Increased	Decreased
Trim	More trim drag	Low trim drag
Elevator Pitch	Pitch nose up reduced	Pitch nose down reduced
Fuel Consumption	Increased	Decreased
Range	Decreased	Increased

In order to maintain tailplane and elevator pitch control effectiveness, without creating excessive aerodynamic forces, it is necessary to place limits on the range of allowable movement of the CG The range of CG positions, for a particular aircraft, varies with the mass of that aircraft.

- At higher mass, the pitch control forces required are greater and the CG forward limit is moved rearwards.
- As aeroplane mass reduces, the CG range is increased by moving the forward limit forwards.

Aeroplane manufacturers provide a CG limits envelope In order for the aeroplane to be safely operated, the CG must lie within the flight envelope at all times.

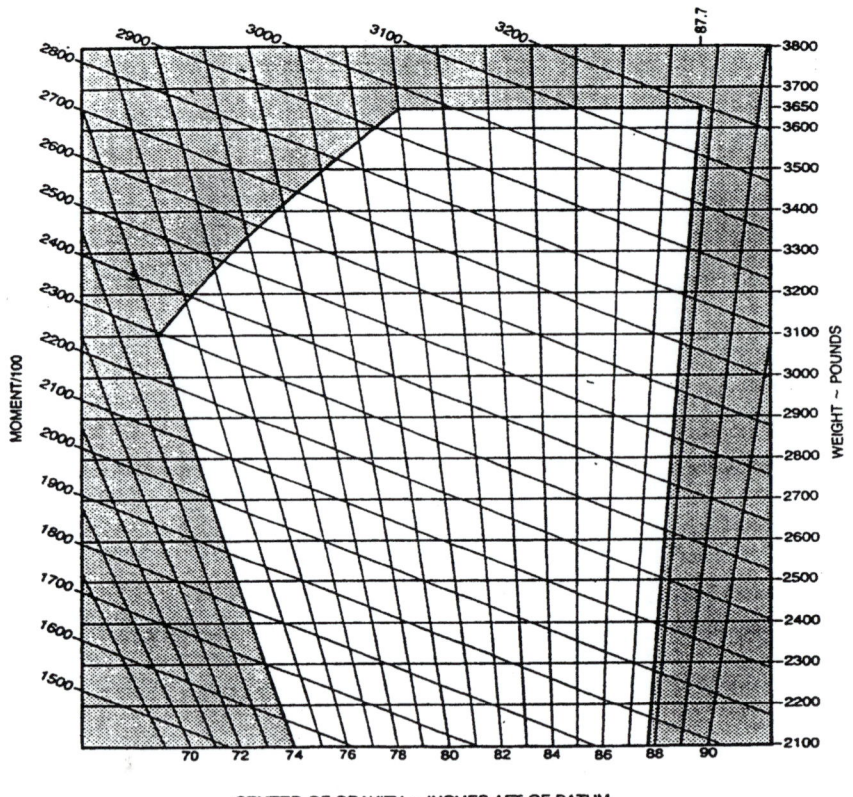

Figure 2.3 Centre of Gravity Envelope

The position of the CG within the envelope affects aeroplane handling:
- A forward CG position results in an increase in stalling speed since a greater downward force must be produced by the tailplane and more lift is required from the wings.
- A forward CG generally results in an increase of stability giving increased static and manoeuvre margins. The aeroplane feels 'heavy' and is less responsive and stick forces for manoeuvring are greater especially during rotation during take-off and whilst flaring during landing.

The position of the CG within the envelope also affects the performance of the aeroplane. A forward CG results in:
- A reduced rate of climb
- A decrease in cruise range
- Increased take off distance with range and endurance being reduced

Pitching moments acting on the aeroplane can be affected by factors which cause the centre of lift to be moved. These factors include:
- Extending or retracting flaps
- Deployment of spoilers
- Flight at supersonic speeds

An aeroplane must be weighed routinely to ascertain its (Basic Empty Mass) BEM prior to initial entry into service and every 4 years in a hangar with the air conditioning switched off and the hangar doors closed, or when new equipment has been added to the aircraft. If fleet masses are used then the aircraft air weighed every 9 years.

A minimum of three points must be used to ascertain the Basic Empty Mass (BEM) of an aircraft

2.1 Determination of CG

2.1.1 Definitions

CG Limits: The range of movement of the CG fore and aft of a datum that does not put the aeroplane in an unsafe condition.

Moment arm / balance arm: The distance from the datum to the centre of gravity of a mass is known as the moment arm

Datum: Chosen on the longitudinal axis of an the aeroplane, but not necessarily between the nose and the tail of the aircraft

These definitions may also be found in the CAP 696.

EASA STUDY GUIDES

MASS & BALANCE

Mass and Balance Self Assessment Test 01

1. The centre of gravity of a body is that point:
A) where the sum of the moments from the external forces acting on the body is equal to zero
B) where the sum of the external forces is equal to zero
C) which is always used as datum when computing moments
D) through which the sum of the forces of all masses of the body is considered to act

2. The stalling speed of an aeroplane will be highest when it is loaded with a:
A) low gross mass and forward centre of gravity
B) low gross mass and aft centre of gravity
C) high gross mass and aft centre of gravity
D) high gross mass and forward centre of gravity

3. With the centre of gravity on the forward limit which of the following is to be expected?
A) A tendency to yaw to the right on take-off
B) A decrease in range
C) A decrease in the landing speed
D) A decrease of the stalling speed

4. If nose wheel moves aft during gear retraction, how will this movement affect the location of the centre of gravity (CG) on the aeroplane?
A) It will cause the CG to move forward
B) The CG location will change, but the direction cannot be told the information given
C) It will cause the CG to move aft
D) It will not affect the CG location

5. The centre of gravity location of the aeroplane is normally computed along the:
A) longitudinal axis
B) lateral axis
C) vertical axis
D) horizontal axis

EASA STUDY GUIDES

MASS & BALANCE

Mass and Balance Self Assessment Test 01 ANSWERS

1	D
2	D
3	B
4	C
5	A

CHAPTER 3
STABILITY

3.1 Definition: Static and Dynamic Stability

3.1.1 Static stability

Stability is defined as the capability of a body to return to its original condition after a disturbance.

> Stability is the capability of a body to return to its original condition after a disturbance

There are three types of static stability, positive, neutral and negative static stability. A body has positive static stability when it returns to its previous condition after a disturbance.

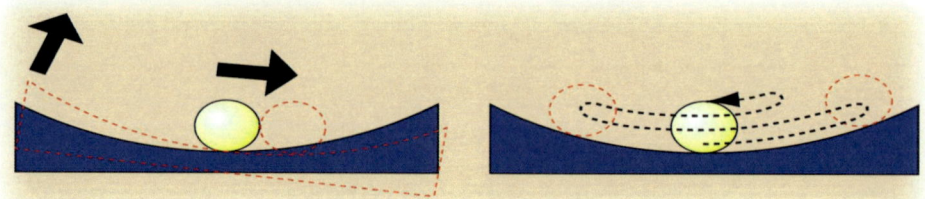

Figure 3.1 Positive static stability

The second type is neutral static stability. A body has neutral or indifferent static stability when it maintains its new position after a disturbance.

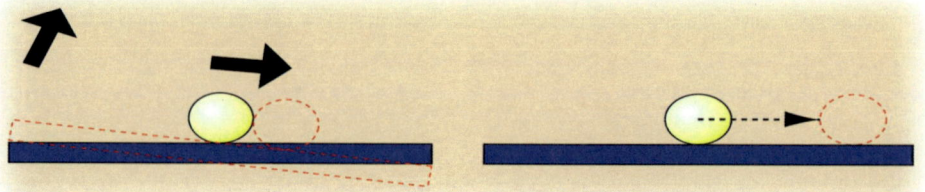

Figure 3.2 Neutral static stability

The third type is negative static stability. A body has negative static stability when it continues to move away from its previous condition after a disturbance.

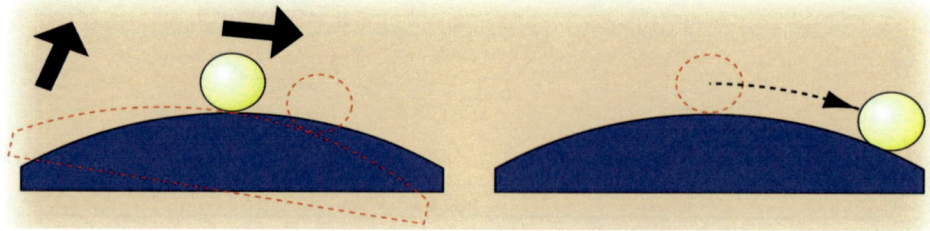

Figure 3.3 Negative static stability

> Static stability is:
> Positive when a body returns to its original condition after a disturbance
> Neutral when it maintains its new position
> Negative when it continues to move away from its previous condition

An aircraft must have positive static stability. For example in turbulence, the aircraft must be able to follow its flight path without allowing rough air to provoke any significant change to its flight path.

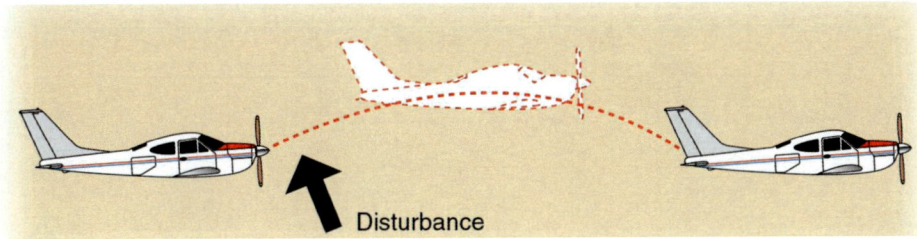

Figure 3.4 Positive static stability is desired in aircraft

This must happen without any intervention from the pilot and with no variations in the position of the control surfaces.

3.1.2 Dynamic stability

Consider a system that is statically stable. One possibility is that, having been displaced from equilibrium, the system will, under the action of the forces created, simply subside back to its original condition, and remain there. Such a system is said to be dynamically stable with aperiodic damping.

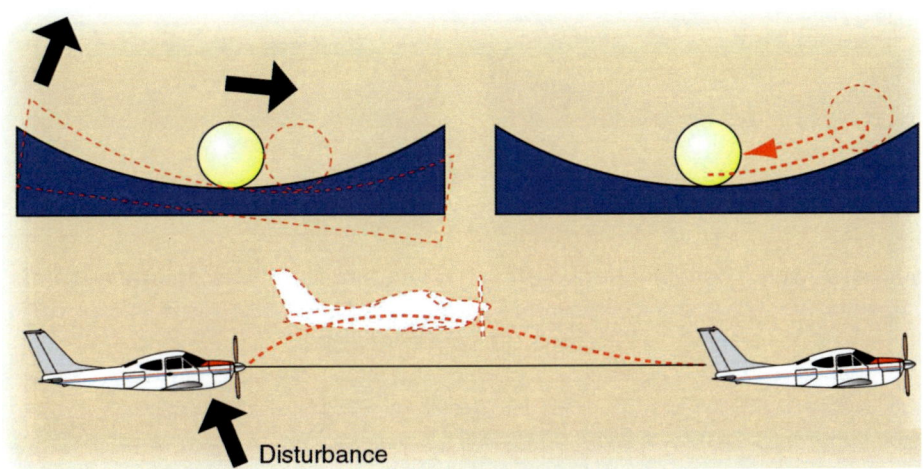

Figure 3.5 Dynamically stable with aperiodic damping

However, the system may, when it reaches the equilibrium point, do so with a certain velocity, so that it overshoots. The new forces will now, since it is statically stable, retard the system, so that a sequence of oscillations occurs in a periodic motion.

A statically stable aircraft affected by a disturbance will oscillate around its intended flight level.

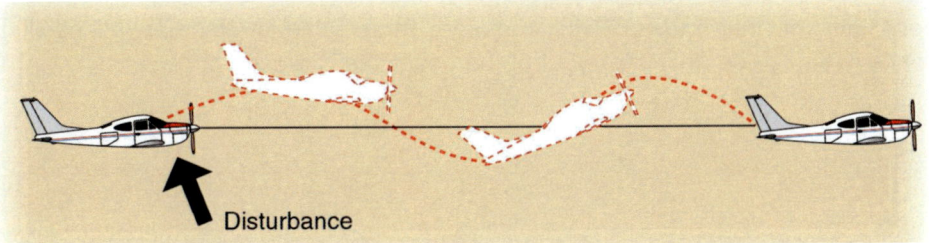

Figure 3.6 Periodic oscillations around a flight level

Dynamic stability describes how and if a body returns to its previous condition after a disturbance

If the period remains the same in length, and the amplitude continues to decrease, the dynamic stability is defined as positive.

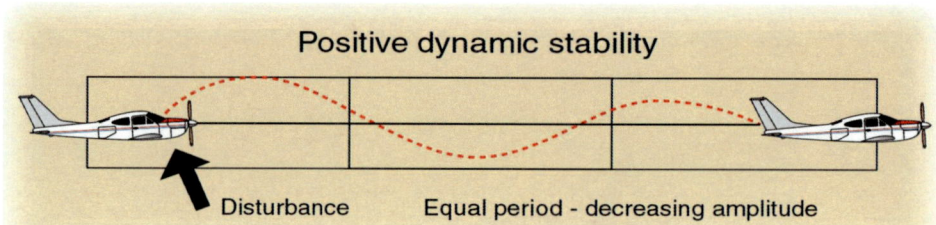

Figure 3.7 Positive Dynamic Stability

A body has positive dynamic stability when it returns to its initial condition through a sequence of periodic (equal time) oscillations of decreasing amplitude

Consider the system with the ball in the bowl. It has positive static stability. As soon as the body starts to move, continue to rock the bowl so that the oscillations do not decrease. Because of the externally applied rocking force, the oscillation of the ball maintains constant amplitude: the body has neutral dynamic stability.

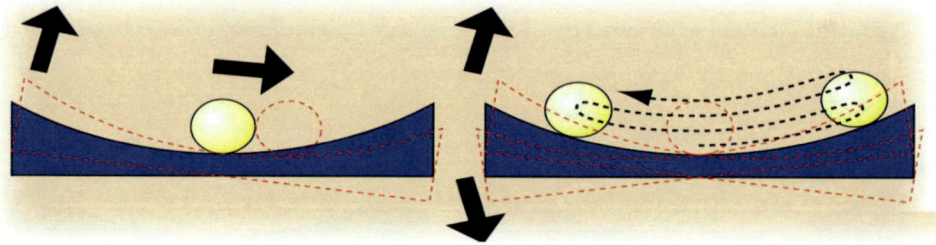

Figure 3.8 Neutral Dynamic Stability

An aircraft that oscillates with a constant period and constant amplitude has neutral dynamic stability.

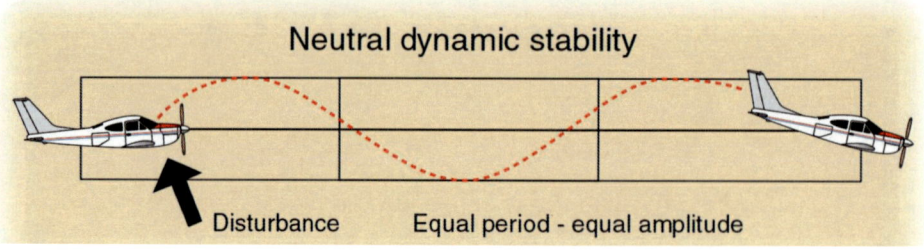

Figure 3.9 Neutral dynamic stability

An aircraft has neutral dynamic stability when its oscillations continue without any change in amplitude

Consider the bowl with the ball and rock the container more violently so that the oscillations of the ball continue to increase in amplitude until it flies out of the bowl: this is a case of negative dynamic stability.

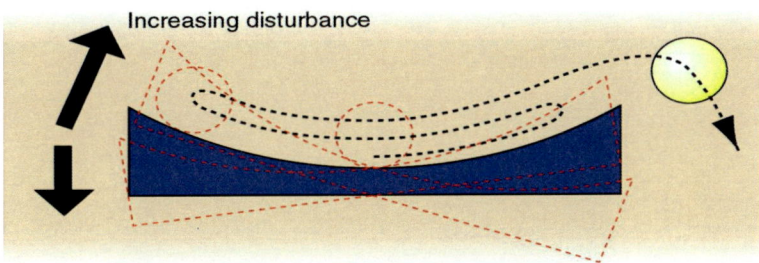

Figure 3.10 Negative dynamic stability

An aircraft that oscillates with constant periods but with increasing amplitude after the disturbance, has negative dynamic stability

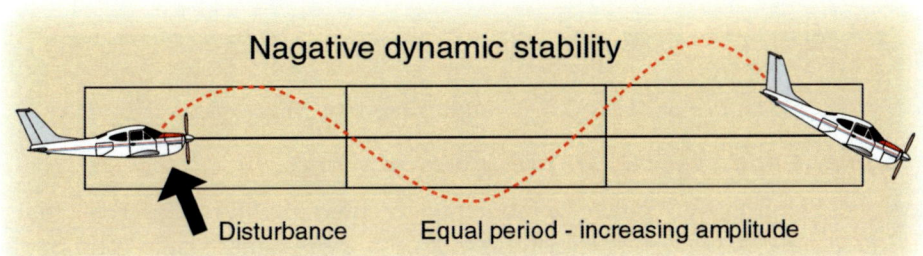

Figure 3.11 Negative dynamic stability

An undamped oscillation cannot be acceptable for an aircraft. The normal requirement is that after one oscillation the Angle of Attack should only be one tenth of that at the beginning of the disturbance and that the oscillations should be completely damped after approximately two oscillations. In other words: a normal aircraft has both positive static stability and positive dynamic stability. Some modern jet fighters are designed to have neutral aerodynamic static stability.

3.1.3 Centre of gravity and centre of pressure

In physics, the centre of gravity is defined as the point where the weight vector of a body is positioned. This is the first important aspect of the centre of gravity; the second is that it is the point around which a body rotates if disturbed.

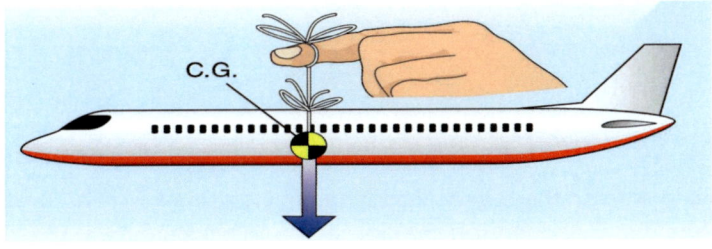

Figure 3.12 Centre of Gravity

The centre of gravity (CG) is the central point of the exerted weight and the centre of rotation of a body.

The location of the centre of gravity with respect to the neutral point determines the longitudinal stability of an aeroplane

To study stability in greater depth, we shall apply our general knowledge of physics to the field of aeronautics. Consider an isolated wing profile when immersed in airflow. The centre of pressure is the point of application of the aerodynamic force. The centre of pressure (CP) changes its position at different A.o.A and moves towards the leading edge when the angle of attack increases.

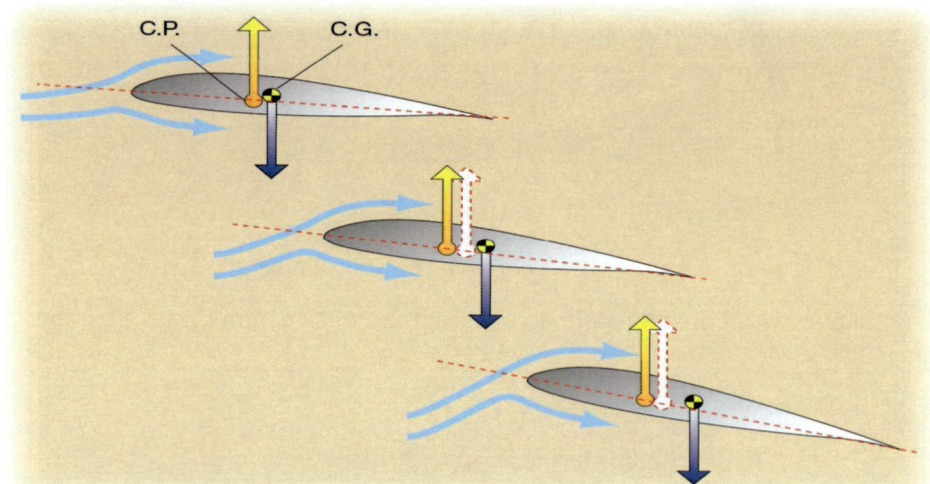

Figure 3.13 The CP changes its position with A.o.A.

3.1.4 Moment and stability of the isolated wing

When the CP does not coincide with the CG a moment is created and the aerofoil will tend to rotate around the CG making it negatively stable. However, the effect on a three-dimensional wing depends on the wing planform and the spanwise aerofoil section. At every section along the wing span, the CP may have different locations.

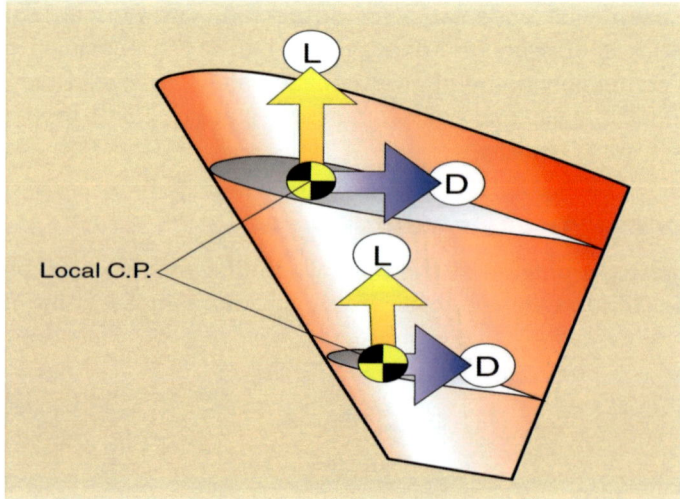

Figure 3.14 Local CP

The effect on the whole wing acts on the mean Aerodynamic Centre, (AC). The turning moment of an isolated wing ($M_{a.c.w}$) is thus dependent on the location of the AC in relation to the CG of the wing.

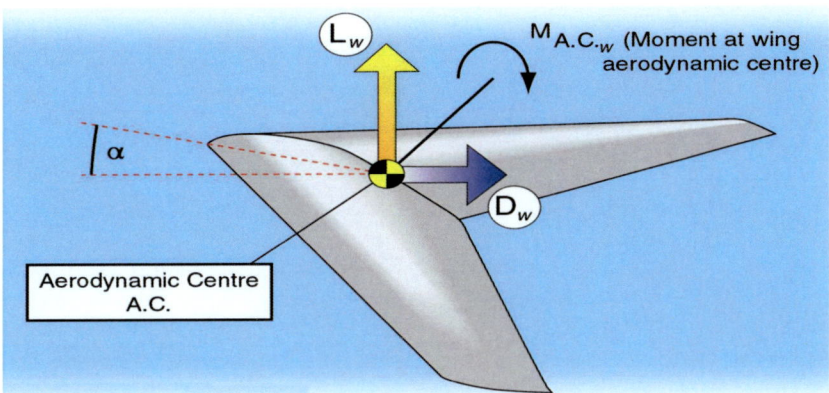

Figure 3.15 Aerodynamic Centre

When the AC is located in front of the CG as A.o.A. is increased the CP will move forward creating a greater pitch up turning moment; the aerofoil will rotate in an unstable manner.

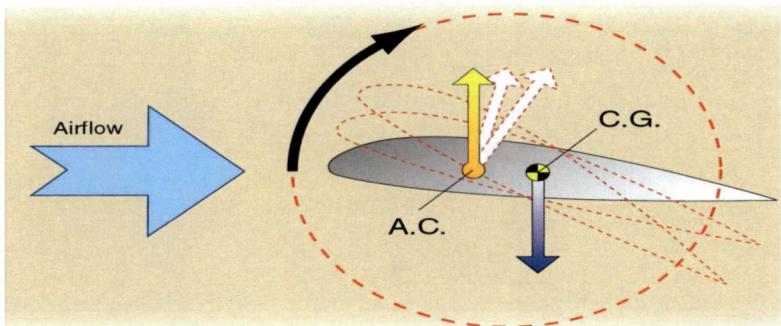

Figure 3.16 Pitch up turning moment with AC is in front of CG

The turning moment around the CG is the product of the force multiplied by the distance between the CG and the AC As a formula: Moment = Force x Arm.

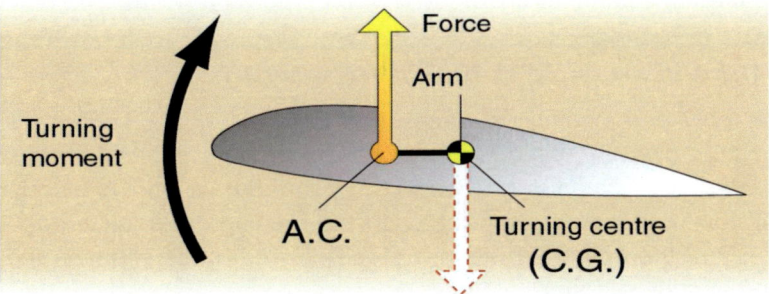

Figure 3.17 An isolated wing appears unstable with the AC in front of the CG

In this situation the aerodynamic force produces a moment, which will cause the profile to rotate so as to increase the angle of attack. This phenomenon causes an increase in the intensity of lift. This, in turn, causes a further increase in the value of the moment. With an isolated wing we therefore have an unstable situation.

If we change the turning centre so that it lies in front of the A.C. of the wing, we will get a new situation. The wing will act as a vane. If the A.o.A increases, a turning moment is created that forces the wing to resume its earlier A.o.A, which will finally change the wing to a new attitude.

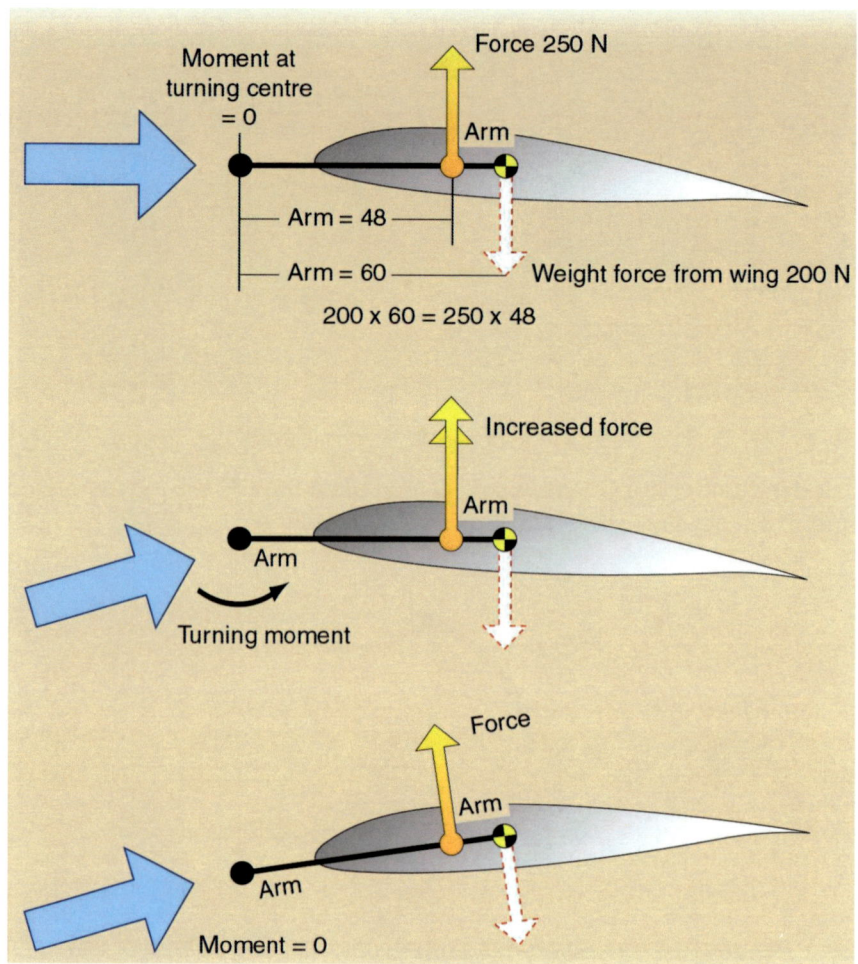

Figure 3.18

With the turning centre in front of the lift force, the wing will appear to be stable

3.1.5 Moment and stability of the entire aircraft

The wings are not the only aerodynamic surfaces that create turning moments. The fuselage and tail surfaces also generate their own CP, which varies with different A.o.A. As a consequence the CP of the entire aircraft may be differently located in relation to the CP of the wings. Consequently, when designing a statically stable aircraft, the wing has to be located on the fuselage in such a position that the CG of the entire aircraft is at the CP of the entire aircraft in a steady flight. In this situation the sum of all forces and moments is zero and the aircraft is in trim.

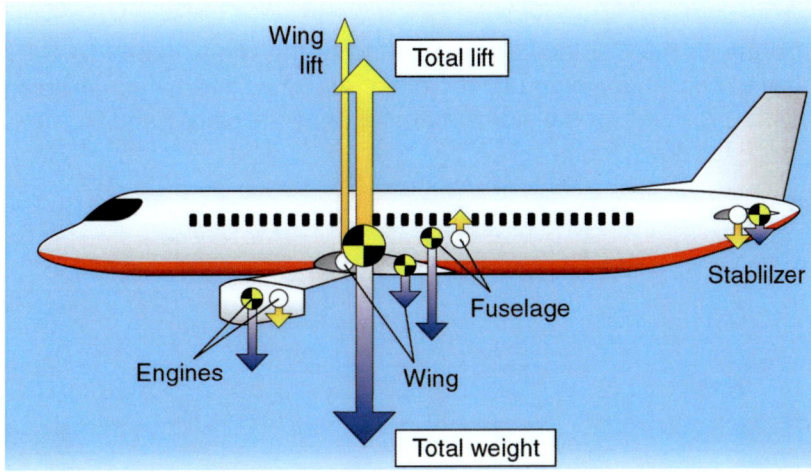

Figure 3.19 An aircraft has many individual CPs

On a statically stable aircraft, the AC of the entire aircraft has to be located behind the total CG of the aircraft. In this situation where the total CG is in front of AC an increased A.o.A. will increase the lift which turns the nose down, thus decreasing the A.o.A. It will also reduce the lift to what it was before the disturbance. In this situation the aircraft is statically stable.

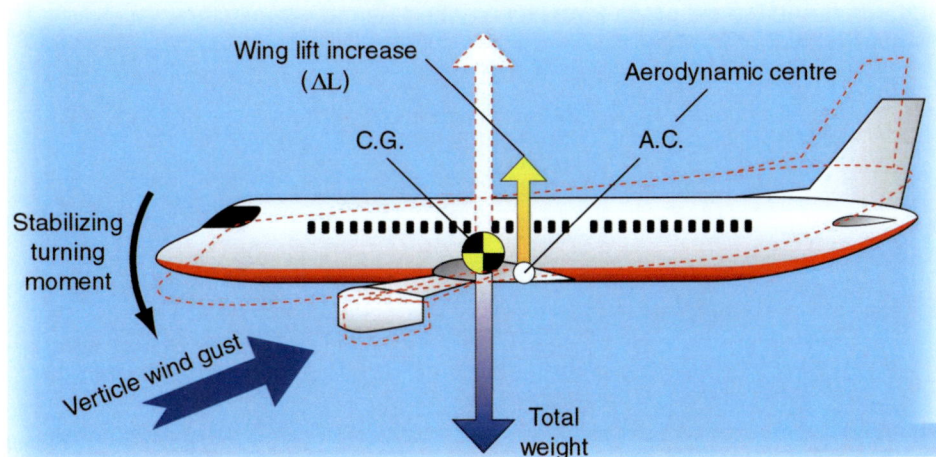

Figure 3.20 An upgust generates more lift and the aircraft pitches down

> In order to have a stable aircraft, the aircraft CG must be in front of the AC

> Aircraft usually have positive static stability with the aircraft CG forward of the AC

3.2 Longitudinal Stability

Longitudinal stability is measured in the fore – aft axis.

3.2.1 Definition of the tailplane as main stabilising factor

To be longitudinally stable, an aircraft must have the tendency to return to trimmed angle of attack after any disturbance without being influenced by the pilot. In the case of conventional aircraft the horizontal stabiliser provides the main stabilising force. Depending on where the centre of gravity is positioned with respect to the wing / fuselage centre of pressure, the tail lift for trim can be either upwards or downwards.

> On a conventional aircraft the horizontal stabiliser provides the main stabilising force

In straight and level flight with the CG located well ahead of the wing / fuselage C.P. the normal moment around the CG is nose-down. To maintain level flight there must be an equal balancing moment in the opposite direction. This is provided by the horizontal stabiliser (tailplane) and is a product of the distance between the CG is and the tail down force.

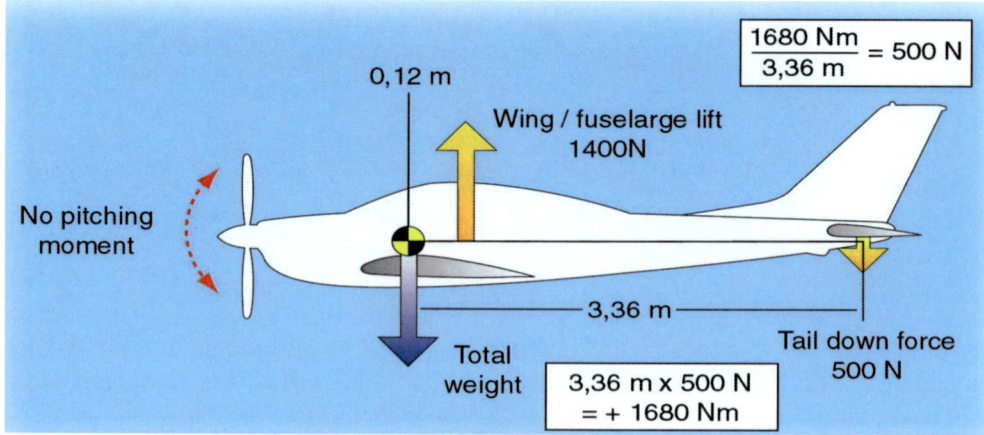

Figure 3.21

The weight of the aircraft and the tail down force is balanced by the wing lift.

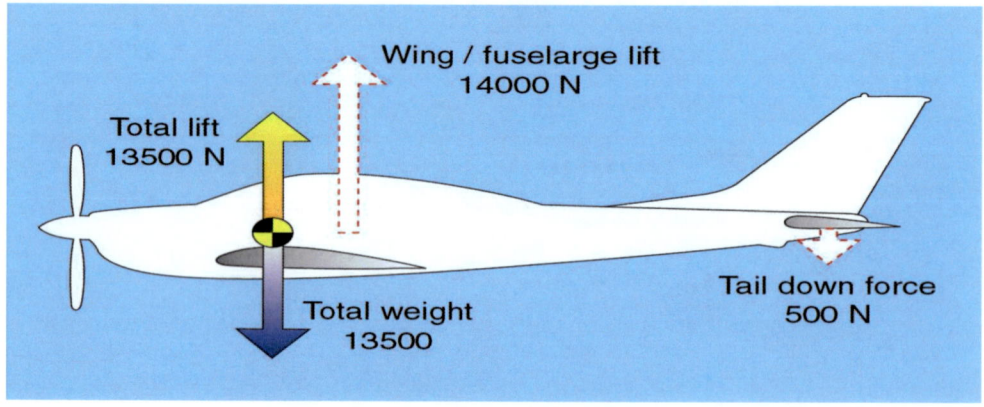

Figure 3.22 Balanced forces

Now assume that the aircraft is hit by a gust so that the angle of attack for both the wings and the stabiliser changes. The wing / fuselage lift increases and the downward force of the stabiliser is reduced. The nose down moment of the wing will therefore increase and the stabiliser 'nose up' moment will decrease. The net result for the statically stable aircraft is a nose-down moment because of the change in total lift (ΔL), which acts at the aerodynamic centre AC and which brings the aircraft back to its original angle of attack.

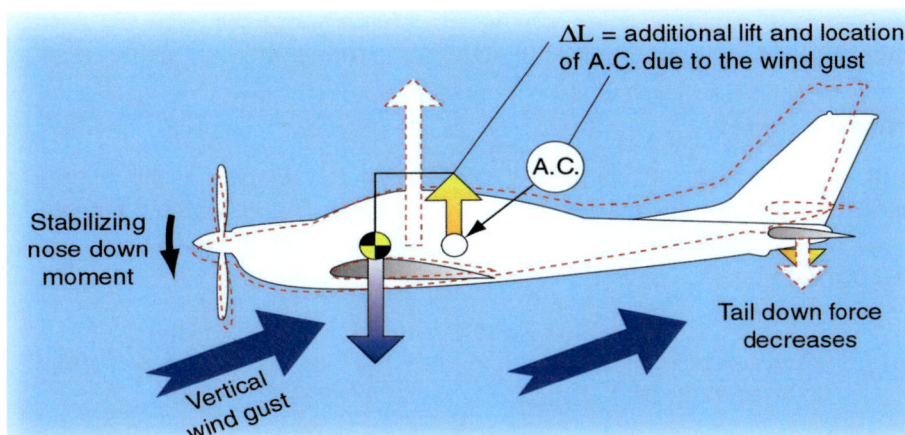

Figure 3.23 Balancing forces with a gust (CG forward of CP))

When the CG lies behind the wing / fuselage CP the wing lift causes a nose-up moment. In order to balance this, the stabiliser, now having a shorter arm, must produce a relatively higher upward force to produce a nose-down moment, higher than the nose-up moment of the wing. This is a less desirable situation.

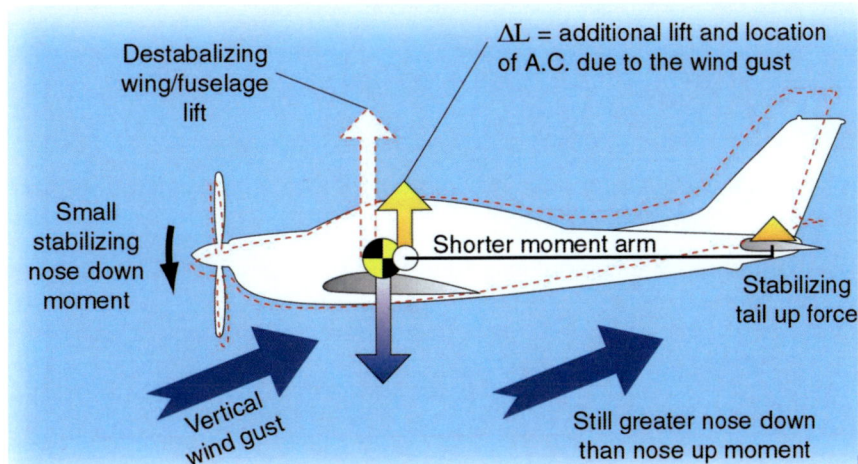

Figure 3.24 CG aft of CP is less desirable

When the CG is located at the same position as the AC, the tailplane may still give a large upward force, but the change in total lift (ΔL), that acts at the AC will not produce any turning moment. With respect to the moments around the CG a disturbance from a wind gust produces no turning moment.

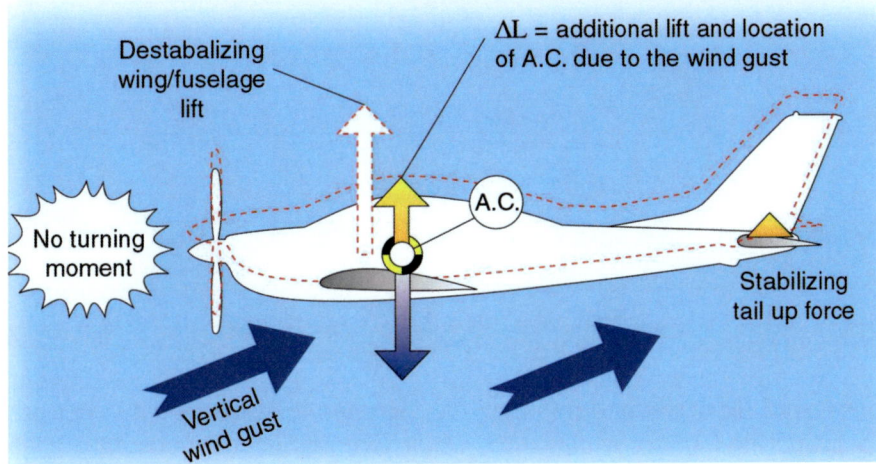

Figure 3.25 No turning moment when CG coincides with CP

If the CG has the same position or is aft of the AC of the wing, the wing / fuselage lift produces a destabilising moment and the moment arm for the stabiliser is reduced.

3.2.2 Neutral point

When the CG is at a certain position compared to the wing / fuselage CP the aircraft will not receive a sufficiently stabilised moment from the tail surface. It will remain in the new attitude instead of turning back to its previous position. Consequently, when the CG is located too far aft of the CP of the wing, the CG and AC of the aircraft could coincide and the aircraft will be neutrally static stable.

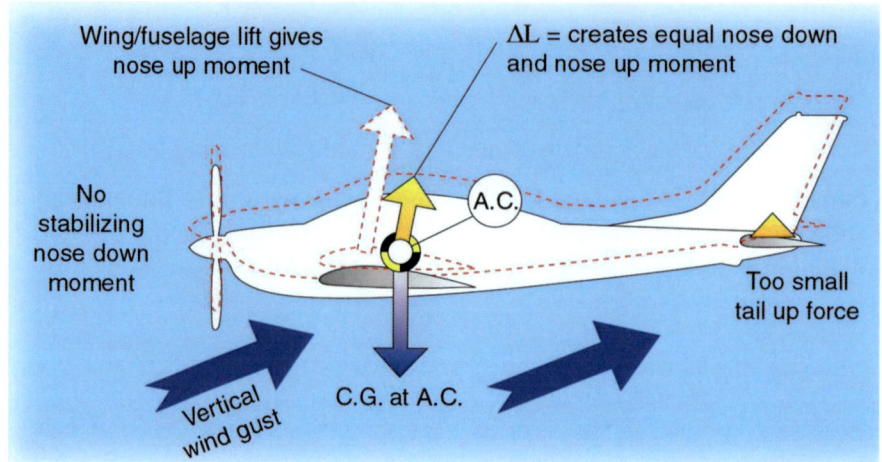

Figure 3.26 There is insufficient stabilising nose down moment with a gust when the AC coincides with the CG so the aircraft remains in the new position

Consequently, the point along the longitudinal axis where the position of the CG causes neutral or indifferent stability is called the Neutral Point.

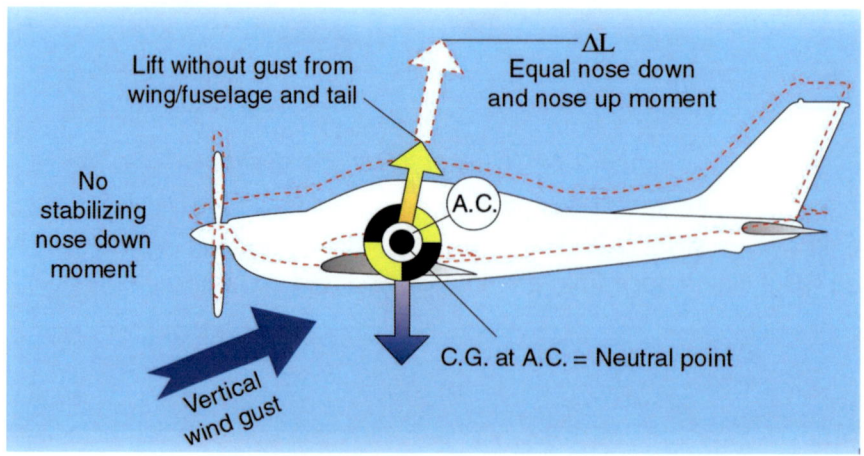

Figure 3.27 The neutral point

> The point along the longitudinal axis where the position of the CG causes neutral stability is called the Neutral point

> An aeroplane that is neutrally stable is caused by a CG which is towards the rearward limit

When the CG is positioned aft of the neutral point, the increase in stabiliser lift is not great enough, thus a destabilising moment is created. In this situation the whole aircraft becomes unstable. It will pitch up, causing a higher A.o.A which creates a further increase in lift and a greater nose up moment. An unstable aircraft shows a natural tendency to diverge from the trimmed flight attitude.

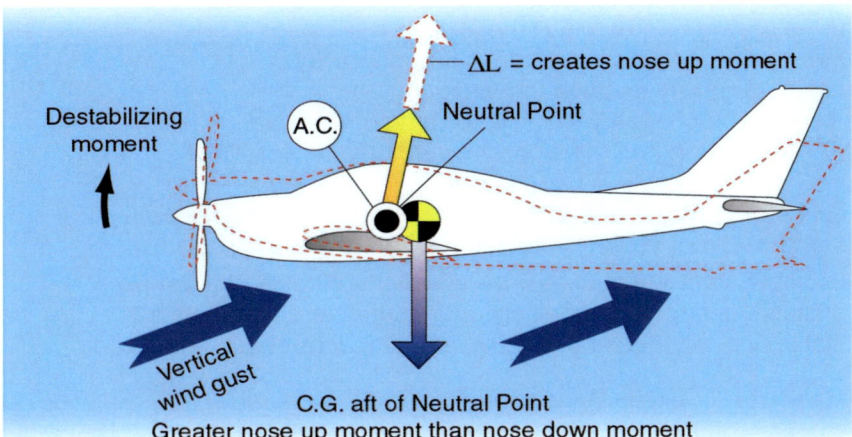

Figure 3.28

If you try to use elevator you may not be able to provide the correct moment at the correct time. The elevator will become too light and sensitive and the aircraft will eventually go out of control. Consequently, as the position of the centre of gravity moves aft, the longitudinal stability is reduced and the aircraft may become dangerously unstable.

> If the CG is positioned behind the neutral point, the aircraft is statically unstable

Mass and Balance Self Assessment Test 03

1. An aeroplane is said to be 'neutrally stable'. This is likely to:
A) be totally unrelated to the position of the centre of gravity
B) cause the centre of gravity to move forwards
C) be caused by a centre of gravity which is towards the rearward limit
D) be caused by a centre of gravity which is towards the forward limit

2. When the centre of gravity is at the forward limit, an aeroplane will be:
A) extremely stable and require small elevator control to change pitch
B) extremely unstable and require excessive elevator control to change pitch
C) extremely unstable and require small elevator control to change pitch
D) extremely stable and will require excessive elevator control to change pitch

3. An aeroplane is loaded with its centre of gravity towards the rear limit. This will result in:
A) a reduced fuel consumption as a result of reduced drag
B) an increase in longitudinal stability
C) a reduction in power required for a given speed
D) an increased risk of stalling due to a decrease in tailplane moment

4. The mass displacement caused by landing gear extension:
A) does not create a longitudinal moment
B) creates a pitch-down longitudinal moment
C) creates a longitudinal moment in the direction (pitch-up or pitch-down) determined by the type of landing gear
D) creates a pitch-up longitudinal moment

5. In cruise flight, an aft centre of gravity location will:
A) decrease longitudinal static stability
B) increase longitudinal static stability
C) does not influence longitudinal static stability
D) not change the static curve of stability into longitudinal

EASA STUDY GUIDES

MASS & BALANCE

Mass and Balance Self Assessment Test 03 ANSWERS

1	C
2	D
3	D
4	C
5	A

CHAPTER 4
Static Margin and MAC

To assure good longitudinal stability an aircraft is usually designed to avoid the CG being too close to the neutral point. The distance between the CG and the neutral point is a direct measure of the longitudinal static stability. The distance between the CG and the neutral point, expressed as a fraction of the wing Mean Aerodynamic wing Chord (MAC) in %, is called the static margin. The designer defines the Mean Aerodynamic wing Chord (MAC). Its location may be estimated approximately by dividing wing area by wing span.

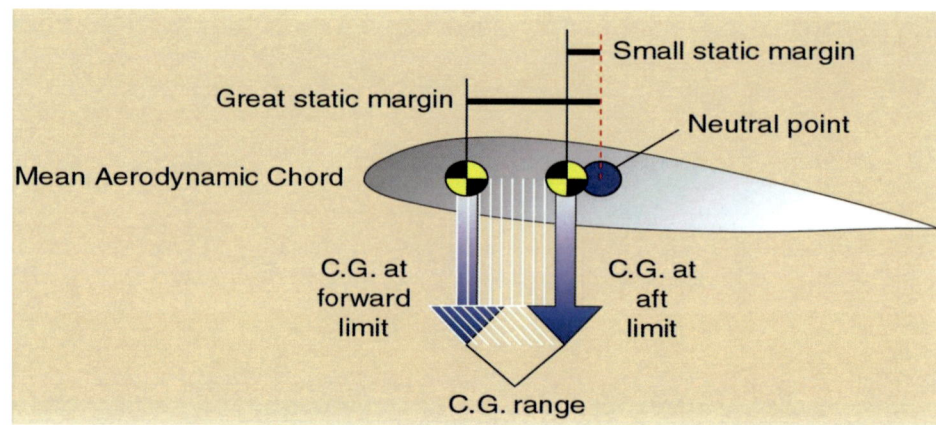

Figure 4.1 Static Margin is the distance from the CG to the neutral point

The distance between the CG and the neutral point is called the static margin and is expressed as a percentage of MAC. A small static margin gives reduced pitch stability and vice versa

4.1.1 Mean Aerodynamic Chord (MAC)

The relationship between Centre of Lift and CG is of great importance. Since the position of the Centre of Lift is related to the chord of the wing it is convenient to refer to the CG position in similar terms. The wing (of a jet transport aircraft) usually has a variable chord.

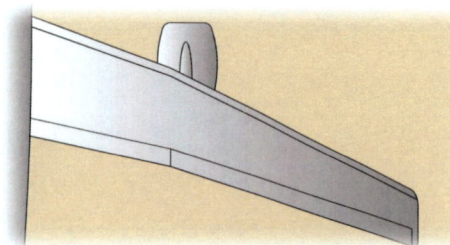

Figure 4.2 Variable Chord length

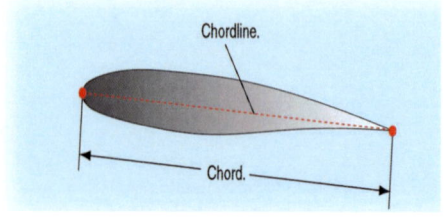

Figure 4.3 Chord line

The average of all the individual chord lengths may be calculated and this is known as the mean aerodynamic chord (MAC).

The length of the MAC and the position of its leading edge in respect of the mass and balance datum are determined by the manufacturer. Details are published in the aeroplane's loading manual. Using this data, the position of the CG can be related to the MAC and given as a % MAC from the leading edge. Percentage (%) mean aerodynamic chord (MAC) is related to the CG as follows.

$$\% \text{ MAC} = \frac{\text{CG position} - \text{Leading edge}}{\text{MAC}} \times 100$$

If distance needs to be calculated (e.g. metres, centimetres) then use the following rearrangement of the equation:

$$\text{MAC} = \frac{\text{MAC}}{100} \times \text{distance the CG is from the leading edge (\%)}$$

4.1.2 Example 1

The aeroplane's CG is established at a point 16.36 m aft of datum
The MAC is 3.416 m and the leading edge of MAC is 15.89 m aft of datum.
Give the position of the C.G. as a % MAC.

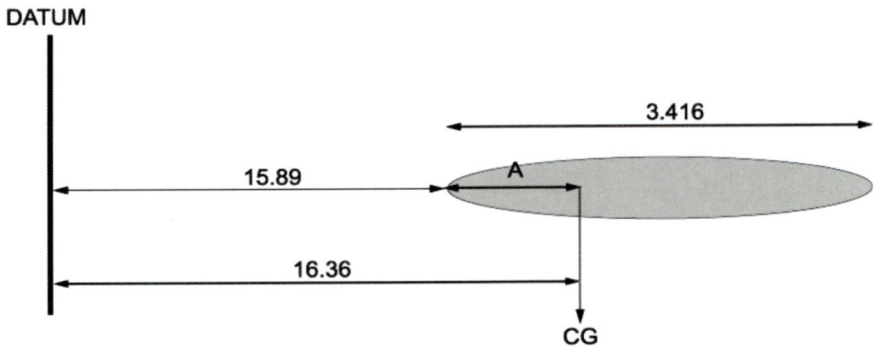

Figure 4.4 MAC Example 1

Solution:

Find distance A:

16.36 m − 15.89 m = 0.47 m

$$\% \text{ MAC} = \frac{100\%}{\text{MAC}} \times (\text{CG Position} - \text{Leading Edge})$$

$$\% \text{ MAC} = \frac{100\%}{3.416 \text{m}} \times (16.36 \text{ m} - 15.89 \text{ m})$$

$$\% \text{ MAC} = \frac{100\%}{3.416 \text{m}} \times 0.47 \text{ m}$$

% MAC = 13.76 %

Example 2

An aeroplane has a mean aerodynamic chord (MAC) of 134.5 inches. The leading edge of this chord is at a distance of 625.6 inches aft of the datum. Give the location of the centre of gravity of the aeroplane in terms of percentage MAC if the mass of the aeroplane is acting vertically through a balance arm located 650 inches aft of the datum:

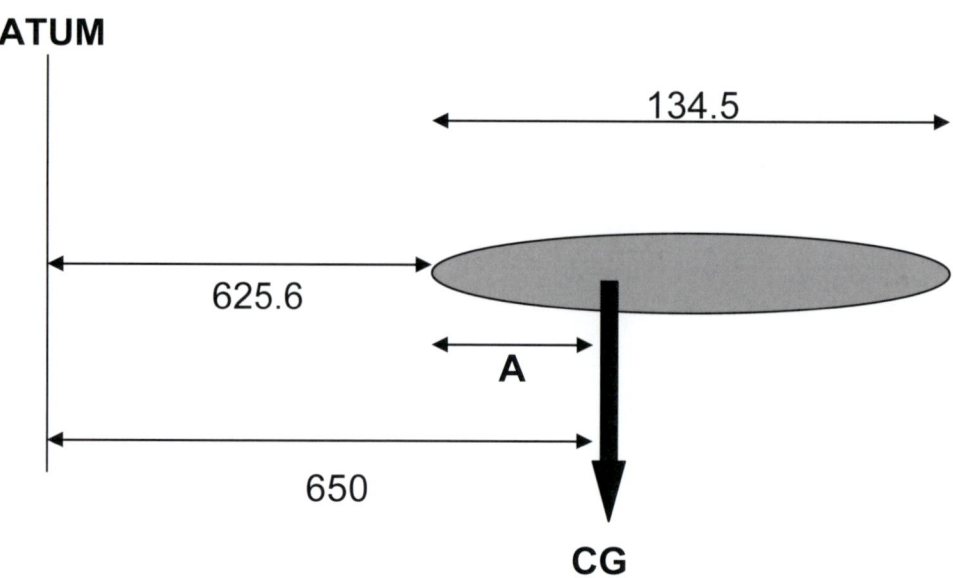

Solution:
Find distance A: 650 − 625.6 = 24.4 % MAC = $\dfrac{100\%}{MAC}$ x (CG position − Leading Edge) % MAC = $\dfrac{100\%}{134.5}$ x (650 − 625.6) % MAC = $\dfrac{100\%}{134.5}$ x 24.4 % MAC = 18.14 %

EASA STUDY GUIDES

MASS & BALANCE

4.2 Practical calculations to Determine CG

Moment: This is the turning effect of a mass around a specified datum and is calculated using the following calculation:

$$\text{Moment} = \text{Mass} \times \text{Arm}$$

The Centre of gravity can be calculated as a distance from the datum using the following equation:

$$\text{CG Distance from datum} = \frac{\text{Total Moment}}{\text{Total Mass}}$$

4.2.1 Example 1

A horizontal beam, 20 m long and considered weightless, has a mass attached at each end; the datum is placed centrally. Fore is to the left and aft to the right. Calculate the position of the C.G. is calculated as follows:

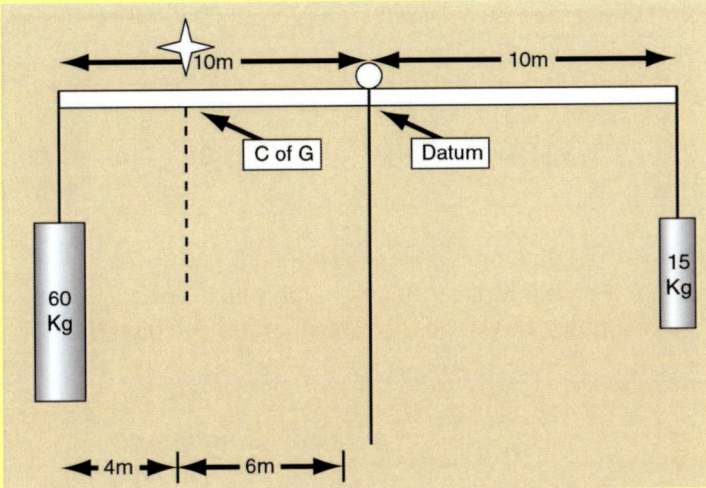

Figure 4.5

Anything aft of the datum is positive and anything ahead of the datum is negative.

Therefore: Moment = Mass x Arm
   Moment (1) = 10 m x 15 kg   Moment (2) = -10 x 60 kg
   Moment (1) = (+) 150   Moment (2) = - 600

Therefore the total moment = (+) 150 – 600 = - 450
Therefore the total mass = 15 kg + 60 kg = 75 kg

Distance from datum = - 450 ÷ 75 kg = - 6 m (forward of datum)

| The reference datum does not need to be on the aircraft when calculating the C.G. |

4.3 Centre of Gravity of an Aeroplane

The next step is to replace the beam with an aeroplane, a typical one with tricycle landing gear. Let us assume that the datum is set at the nose.

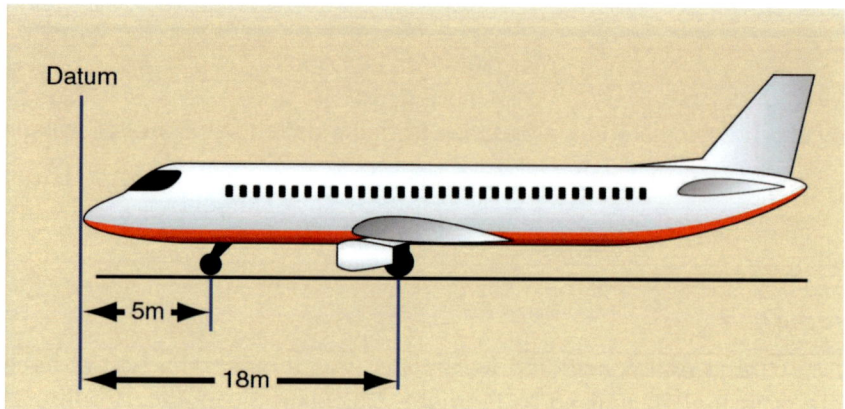

Figure 4.6 Centre of Gravity of an Aeroplane

We are unsure of the position of the Centre of Gravity and are given the following information:

Nose Wheel	=	4000 Newtons (N)	4000 ÷ 9.81 = 407.75 kg
Left Main Wheel	=	5100 Newtons (N)	5100 ÷ 9.81 = 519.88 kg
Right Main Wheel	=	5000 Newtons (N)	5000 ÷ 9.81 = 509.68 kg
Total Mass	=		**1437.31 kg**

- To begin with the three given weights must be converted into kilograms.
- Newtons 2nd law states that: Force = Mass x Acceleration (9.81 m/s^{-2})
- The force and the acceleration are known so the mass can be calculated.

$$\text{Mass (kg)} = \frac{\text{Force (N)}}{\text{Acceleration (m/s)}}$$

We now know all the parameters to calculate the C.G.:

Nose Moment	=	5m x 407.75 kg	=	2038.75
Left Main Moment	=	18m x 519.88 kg	=	9357.84
Right Main Moment	=	18m x 509.68 kg	=	9174.54
Total Moment	=		=	**20570.83**

CG Distance From Datum	=	Total Moment ÷ Total Mass
	=	20,570.83 ÷ 1437.31
	=	**(+) 14.31 m**

Therefore the Centre of Gravity is 14.31 m behind the datum

It is stated, in JAR-OPS 1, that an operator shall establish mass and balance documentation prior to each flight. The mass and balance documentation must enable the commander to determine that the load and its distribution is such that the mass and balance limits of the aeroplane are not exceeded.

The person completing the documentation must be named on and must also sign that document. This document must be acceptable to the Commander. Countersigning the document indicates acceptance.

4.4 Fuel Calculations

When calculating the centre of gravity of an aircraft it may be required to convert certain fuel units into kilograms.

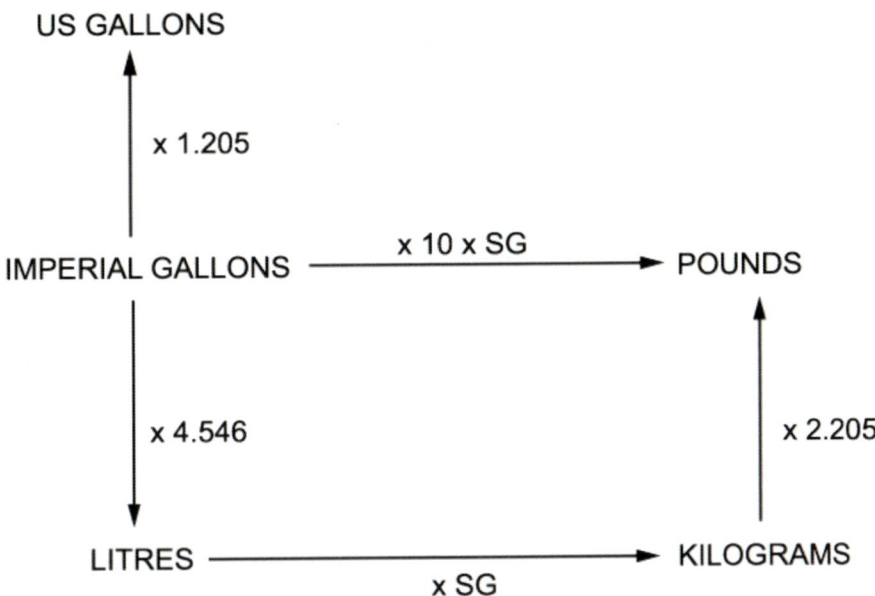

Where SG = specific gravity

Figure 4.7 Fuel Conversions

4.4.1 To convert USG into lbs

> Multiply USG by 6

4.4.2 Calculations with Specific gravity

Water is the reference unit for measuring specific gravity of different liquids and has a specific gravity of 1.0. 1 litre of water has mass of 1 kg. A liquid which is less dense than water will have a specific gravity which is a fraction of 1.0. AVGAS has a specific gravity of 0.72 so if you multiply the volume of AVGAS in litres by its specific gravity of 0.72 the mass of AVGAS may be calculated.

> Example:
> What is the mass of 200 litres of AVGAS assuming a specific gravity of 0.72
>
> 200 litres x 0.72 = 144 kg

EASA STUDY GUIDES

MASS & BALANCE

4.5 Moving the Centre of Gravity

Before flight loads may be moved (or ballast may be added or removed) around to re-position the centre of gravity to within the specified limits. The amount to move can be found out accurately using the following equation:

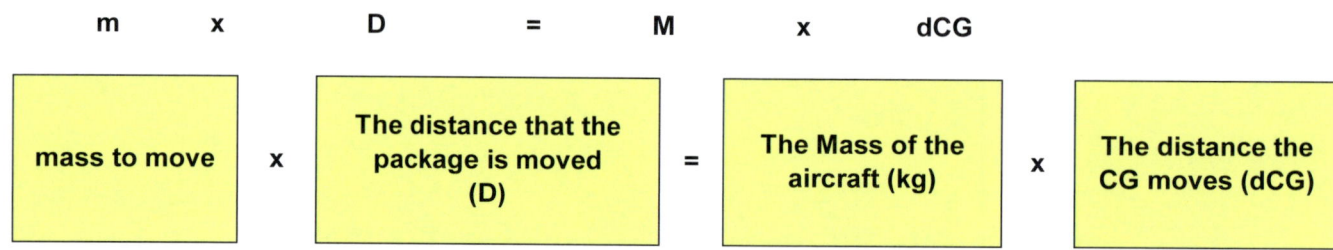

$$m \times D = M \times dCG$$

mass to move × The distance that the package is moved (D) = The Mass of the aircraft (kg) × The distance the CG moves (dCG)

The formula can be used to calculate any one of these four parameters through the use of transposition.

4.5.1 Example 1

The distance between cargo hold A and B is 5 m, with an aircraft BEM of 2000 kg. To move the C.G. by 15 cm, how much mass is required to be moved?

Mass to move   m × 5 = 2000 × 0.15
Therefore: m × 5 = 300
                m   = 300 ÷ 5
                m   = **60 kg needs to be moved**

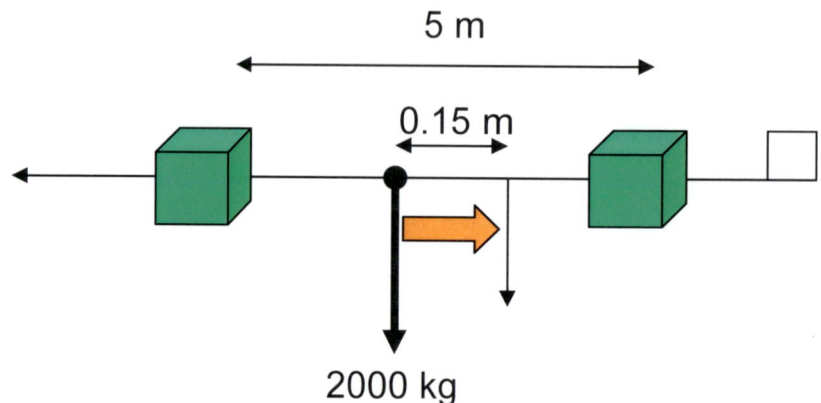

EASA STUDY GUIDES

MASS & BALANCE

How far the CG moves if we shift a certain mass in the aircraft may also be calculated:

4.5.2 Example 1

The distance between cargo hold A and B is 6 m with an aircraft BEM of 3000 kg. A package weighing 30 kg is moved from cargo hold A to B. What effect will this have on the C.G.?

$$
\begin{aligned}
m \times D &= M \times dCG \\
30 \text{ kg} \times 6 &= 3000 \times dCG \\
180 &= 3000 \times dCG \\
dCG &= 180 \div 3000 \\
dCG &= \mathbf{0.06 \text{ m}}
\end{aligned}
$$

The centre of gravity moves aft by 6 cm

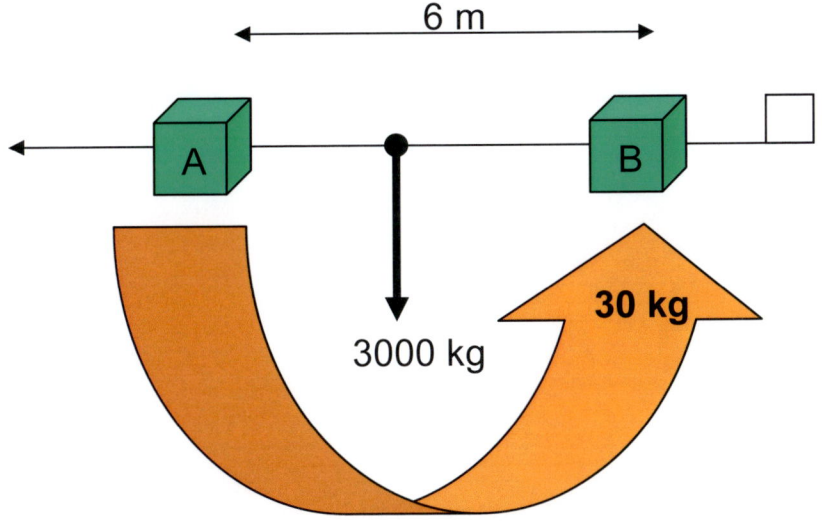

Drawing the above diagram indicates the correct answer. If we move the package is moved aft, since weight acts through the CG, the CG will follow it and move aft. The most likely answer will be a positive number or a number greater number than that for the CG.

4.6 Adding or Removing a Weight

It is sometimes required to calculate how must ballast is required to be placed on the aircraft or removed from the aircraft to bring the CG within its limits. We refer to the technique as the Initial Total Moment method and it utilises the following equation:

New Total Moment = Old Total Moment +/- Additional Moment

New Total Moment = (Aircraft mass +/- additional mass) x the new CG position
Old Total Moment = Aircraft mass x old CG position
Additional Moment = Additional mass x baggage hold arm

4.6.1 Example 1

An aircraft weighs 3000 lbs and the CG is 70 inches aft of datum. The aft CG limit is at 71 in aft of datum. What is the maximum weight that can be loaded into a hold at 110 in aft of the datum to bring the CG to the aft limit?

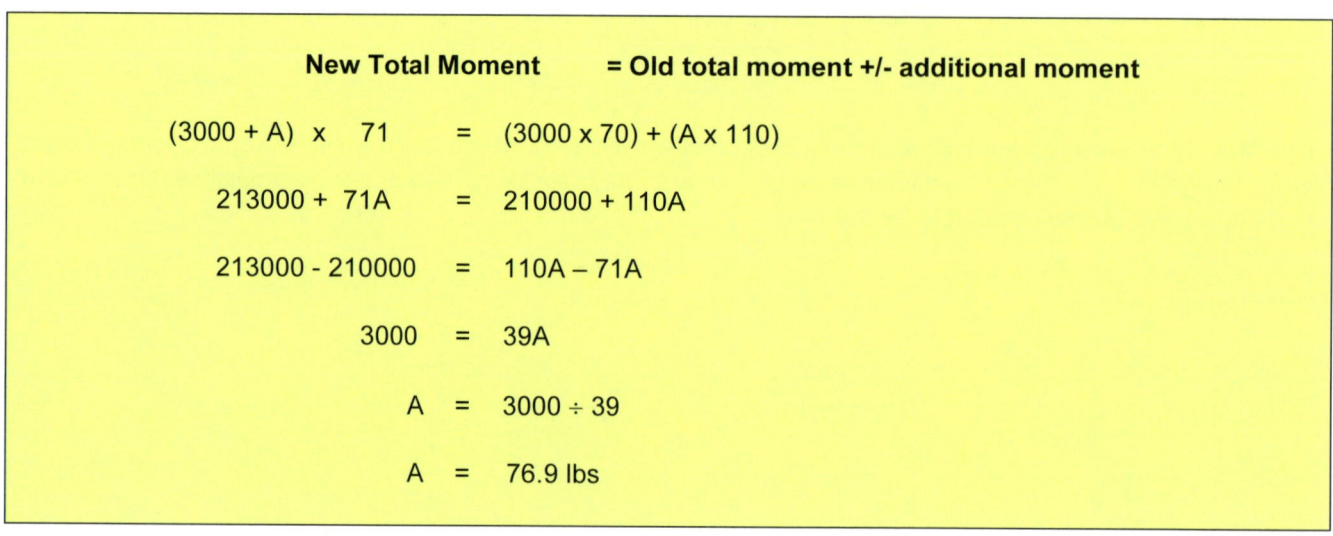

Figure 4.8 Adding a mass

New Total Moment = Old total moment +/- additional moment

(3000 + A) x 71 = (3000 x 70) + (A x 110)

213000 + 71A = 210000 + 110A

213000 - 210000 = 110A − 71A

3000 = 39A

A = 3000 ÷ 39

A = 76.9 lbs

If brackets are used then a rule of thumb is that every number inside the bracket must be multiplied by what is outside the bracket.

Example 2

The mass of an aeroplane is 1950 kg. If 450 kg is added to a cargo hold 1.75 metres from the loaded centre of gravity (CG). The loaded CG will move:

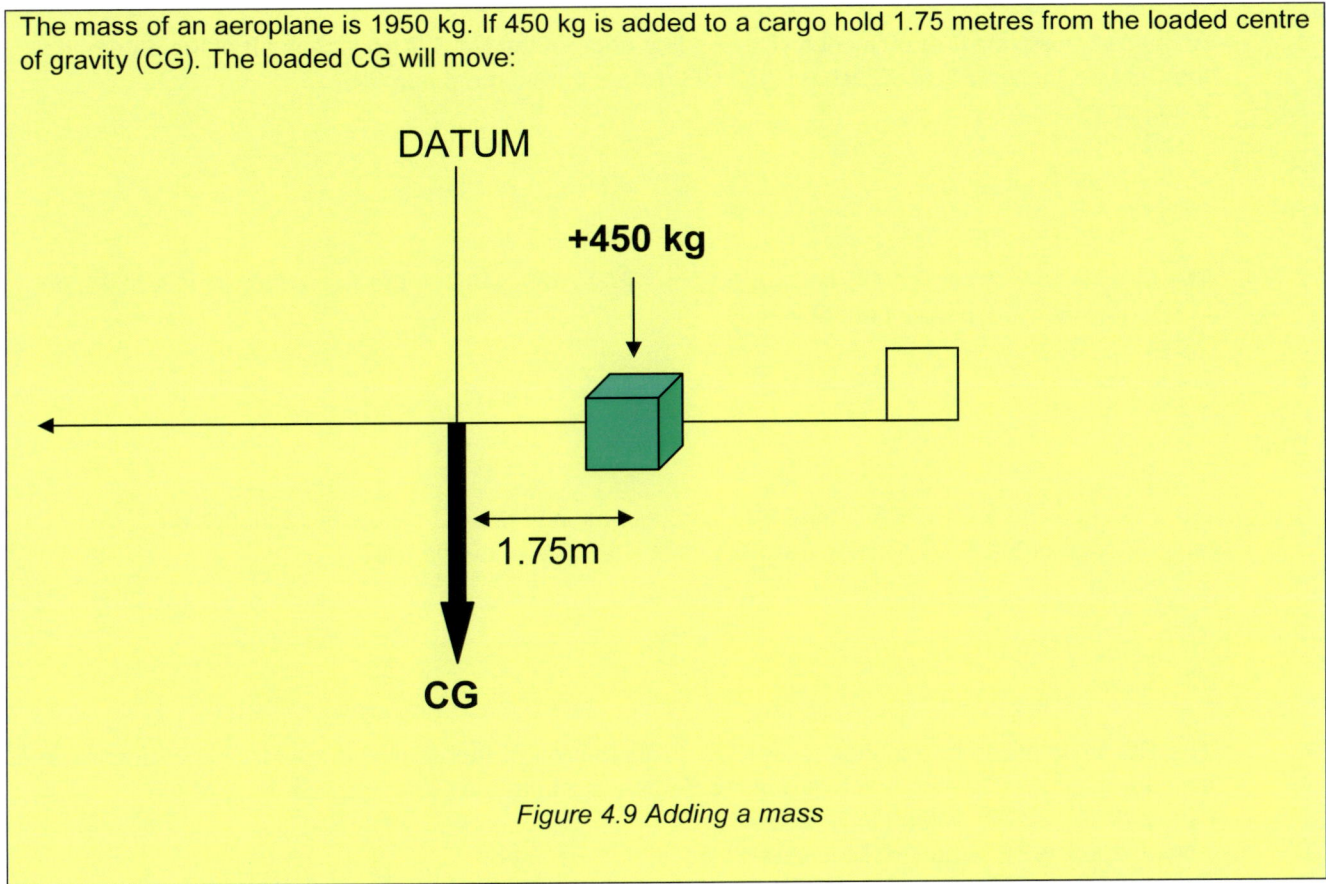

Figure 4.9 Adding a mass

NOTE: If a datum isn't given in the question, assume one and place it on the centre of gravity (CG)

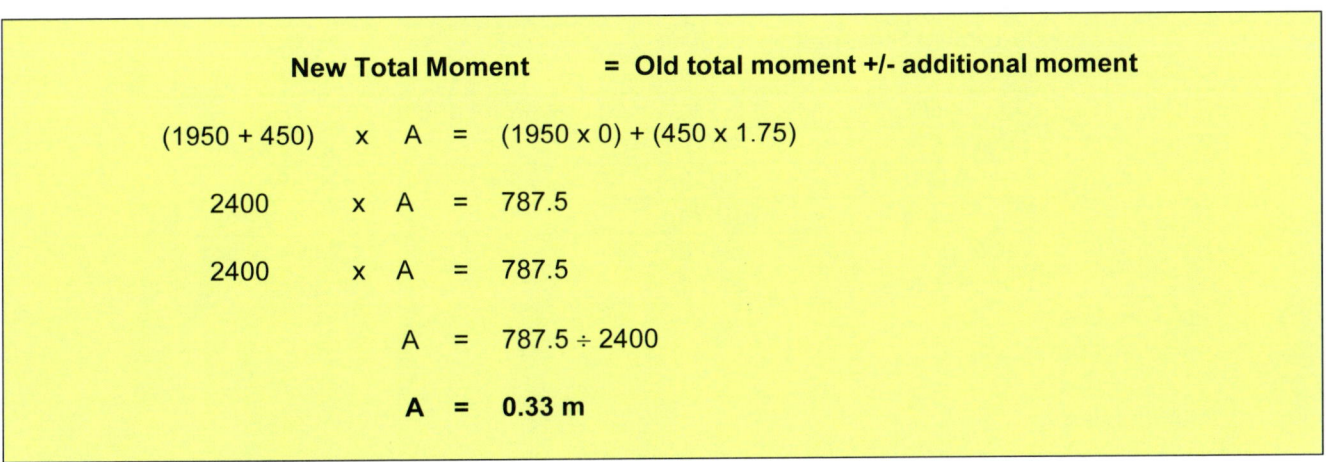

Now to prove that the theory works, try placing the datum in different positions. You will see that every answer you derive will be the same.

EASA STUDY GUIDES

MASS & BALANCE

Mass and Balance Self Assessment Test 04

1. An aircraft has a MAC of 60 inches. The leading edge of the MAC is 15 inches aft of the datum. If the CG position is 18% MAC, what is the CG distance from the datum?
A) 2.58 inches
B) 10.8 inches
C) 25.8 inches
D) 25.8 cm

2. The MAC is 58 inches. The CG limits are from 26% to 43% MAC. If the CG is found to be at 45.5% MAC, how many inches is it out of limits?
A) 2.4 m
B) 2.4 inches
C) 1.4 m
D) 1.4 inches

3. If the CG position is 24% MAC, the MAC is 80 inches, and the CG datum is 17 inches aft of the leading edge of the MAC, what is the CG position relative to the datum?
A) 2.2 inches
B) 19.2 inches
C) 16 inches
D) 1.6 inches

4. The CG limits are from 8 inches forward to 12 inches aft of the datum. If the MAC is 50 inches and its leading edge is 17 inches forward of the datum, what are the CG limits as a % of MAC?
A) Forward limit is 18% and aft limit is 58%
B) Forward limit is 58 % and aft limit is 18%
C) Forward limit is 22% and aft limit is 45%
D) Forward limit is 13% and aft limit is 42%

5. Calculate the position of the C.G. of an aeroplane given the following data:

Maximum Structural Mass	6500 lb	
C.G. limits	5.5 to 1 inch forward of datum	
BEM	4500 lb	3 in forward
Fuel (SG 0.74)	110 Imp	8 in aft
Oil (SG 0.87)	10 Imp	4 in forward
Crew	290 lb	35 in forward
Passenger	290 lb	30 in aft

A) -14.7 metres
B) +14.7 inches
C) +1.47 inches
D) -1.47 inches

6. (Refer to the table in question 5) If the fuel consumption is 32 imp gal / h and the oil consumption is 1 imp gal / h, calculate the new CG after a 2 h flight:
A) +2.28 cm
B) -2.28 inches
C) +2.28 inches
D) -2.28 cm

CRANFIELD AVIATION TRAINING SCHOOL LTD. PART-FCL ATO N° 276
CATS INNOVATION CENTRE, LUTON, Bedfordshire LU2 8DL U.K.   www.catsaviation.com

EASA STUDY GUIDES

MASS & BALANCE

7. The readings on the scales during aircraft weighing are:

Tail Wheel	160 Newtons	5.4 m from datum
Right Main Wheel	320 Newtons	
Left Main Wheel	305 Newtons	

The datum of the aircraft is through the centre of the main wheel.
What is the BEM and the Centre Of Gravity position?

A) BEM 100 kg, C.G. –2.2 m
B) BEM 95 kg, C.G. +2.2 m
C) BEM 90 kg, C.G. –1.1 m
D) BEM 80 kg, C.G. +1.1 m

8. Given the following:

BEM	2500 kg	+ 0.06 m
Crew	150 kg	-3.45 m
Crew baggage	10 kg	-2.92 m
Fuel	735 kg	-1 m
Passengers	450 kg	0
Forward baggage	140 kg	-4
Aft baggage	175 kg	+2.3

If the fuel consumption for the flight is 425 kg and the Performance Limited Landing Mass is 4000 kg, is the aircraft safe for landing?

A) Yes (LM 3735 kg, C.G. 0.23m)
B) No (LM 3735 kg, C.G. 0.23m)
C) Yes (LM 3525 kg, C.G. 0.23 inches)
D) No (LM 4130 kg, C.G. 0.23 m)

9. An aircraft has a loaded weight of 5500 lb. The CG is 22 inches aft of the datum. A passenger weighing 150 lb moves from row 1 to row 3, a distance of 70 inches. What will be the new position of the CG?

A) 2.39 inches
B) 239 inches
C) 23.9 inches
D) 23.9 cm

10. The CG limits of an aircraft are from 83 inches to 93 inches aft of datum. The CG as loaded is found to be at 81 inches aft of the datum. The loaded weight is 3240 lb. How much weight must be moved from the forward hold, 25 inches, aft of the datum, to the aft hold, 142 inches, aft of the datum, to bring the CG to the forward limit?

A) 45.38 lbs
B) 55.38 lbs
C) 55.38 kg
D) 55.38 ltrs

11. The loaded weight of an aircraft is 12,400 KG. The aft CG limit is (+) 102 inches. If the CG as loaded is (+) 104.5 inches, how many rows forward must two passengers move from the rear seat row (224 inches) to bring the CG on to the aft limit, if the seat pitch is 33 inches (assume a passenger weight is 75 KG each)?

A) 16.8 inches (6 rows)
B) 20.6 inches (6 rows)
C) 206 cm (6 rows)
D) 206 inches (6 rows)

CRANFIELD AVIATION TRAINING SCHOOL LTD. PART-FCL ATO N° 276
CATS INNOVATION CENTRE, LUTON, Bedfordshire LU2 8DL U.K.
www.catsaviation.com

EASA STUDY GUIDES

MASS & BALANCE

12. What is the CG as a percentage of the MAC at the DOM for the aeroplane crewed as shown?

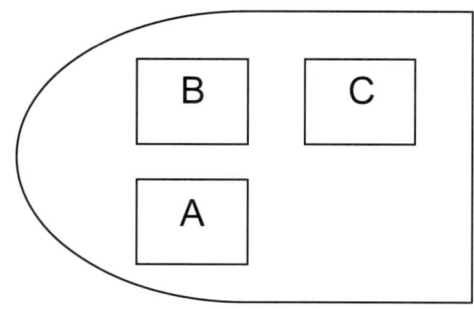

BEM   18000 kg
Pilot   100 kg
1st Officer   90 kg
Flt Engineer   80 kg
Special equipment   1000 kg
MAC   3 m
CG at BEM   16.6 m
CG at BEM   20% MAC

MOMENT TABLE

Seat A or B	Moment
70 kg	-35
80 kg	-40
90 kg	-45
100 kg	-50
110 kg	-55
120 kg	-60
Seat C	
70 kg	+35
80 kg	+40
90 kg	+45
100 kg	+50
110 kg	+55
120 kg	+60
Special Equipment 1000 kg	+15000

A)   9.3%
B)   10.65%
C)   12.0%
D)   21.05%

EASA STUDY GUIDES

MASS & BALANCE

Mass and Balance Self Assessment Test 04 ANSWERS

1   C

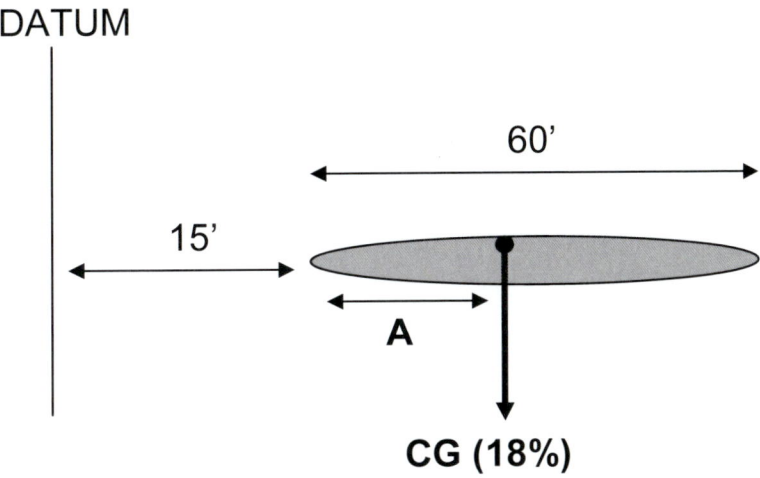

After drawing the diagram calculate 18% of 60 inches.

> MAC = $\dfrac{MAC}{100}$ x distance the CG is from the leading edge (%)

> MAC = (60 ÷ 100) x 18
> MAC = 10.8'
>
> Plus 15' to the answer since the question is asking the distance from datum, not from the leading edge
>
> ANSWER = **25.8' (C)**

EASA STUDY GUIDES

MASS & BALANCE

2   D

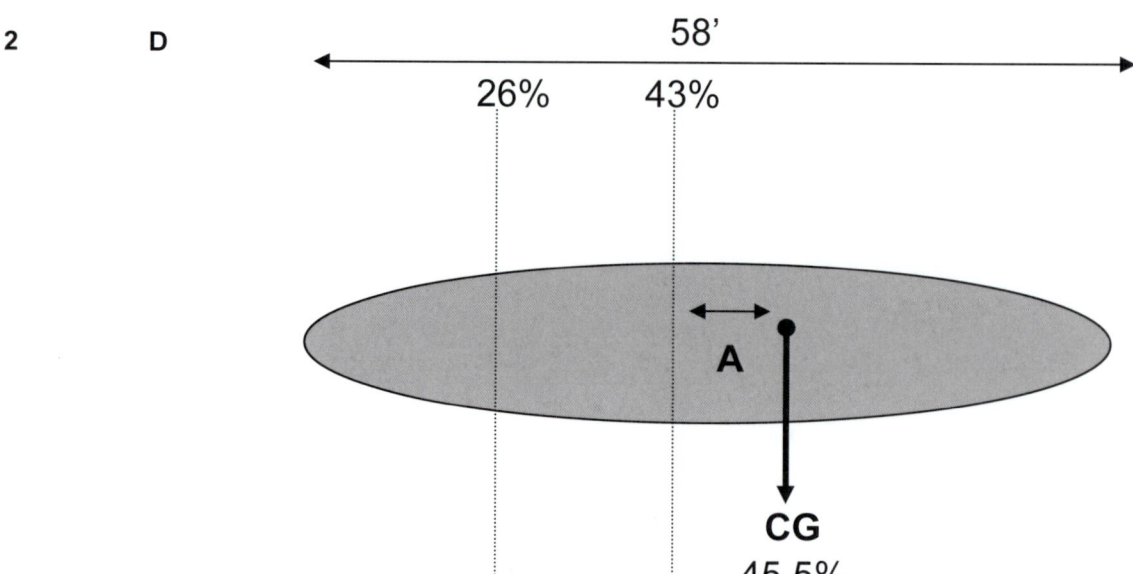

After drawing the diagram you can see that we need to calculate the value of A:

A = 45.5% - 43% = 2.5%

Calculate 2.5% of 58 inches

$$MAC = \frac{MAC}{100} \times \text{distance the CG is from the leading edge(\%)}$$

MAC = (58 ÷ 100) x 2.5
MAC = 1.4 inches

ANSWER = **1.4 inches (D)**

3   A

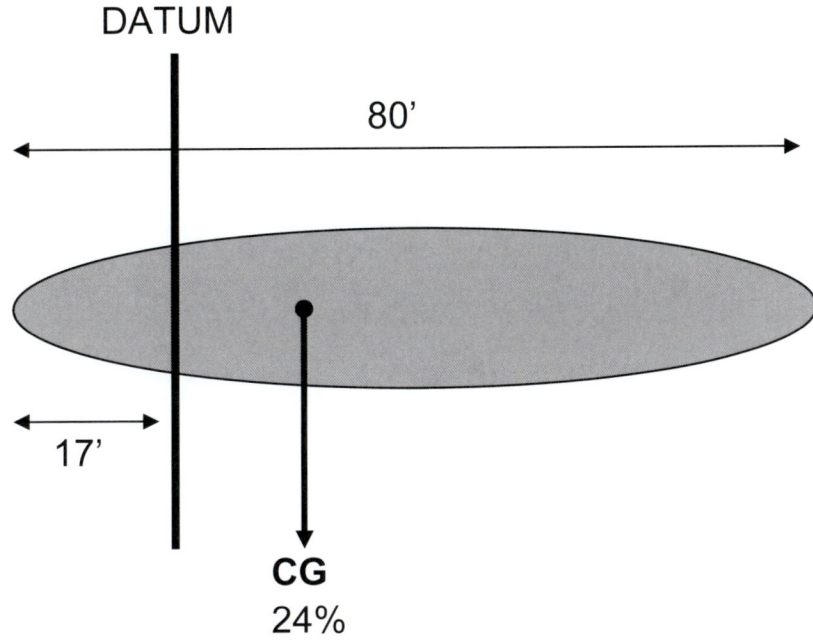

Calculate 24% of 80', which is the centre of gravity with reference to the leading edge.

$$MAC = \frac{MAC}{100} \times \text{distance the CG is from the leading edge (\%)}$$

$$MAC = (80 \div 100) \times 24$$
$$MAC = 19.2 \text{ inches}$$

The question is asking the centre of gravity position in relation to the datum and not the leading edge. Calculate the distance from the datum:

$$MAC = 19.2' - 17'$$

ANSWER = 2.2' (A)

4   A

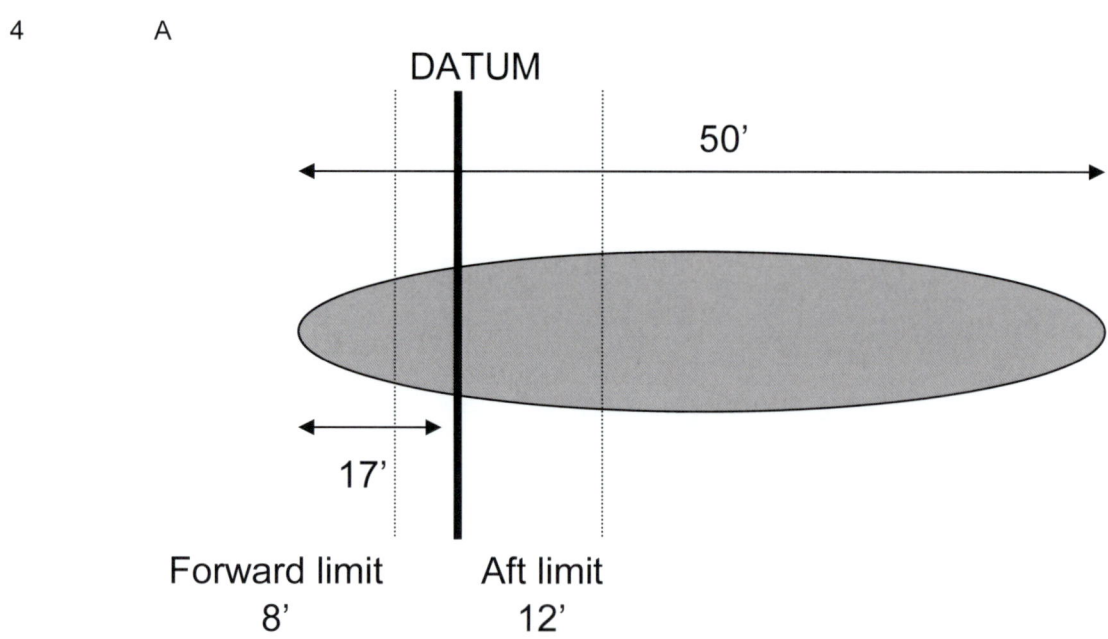

To begin with we must calculate where the forward and aft limits are in relation to the leading edge.

Forward limit: 17 − 8 = **9 inches** aft of the leading edge

Aft limit: 17 + 12 = **29 inches** aft of the leading edge

No we need to calculate what each of these values are as a percentage of MAC.

$$\% \text{ MAC} = \frac{100\%}{\text{MAC}} \times \text{distance the CG is from the leading edge}$$

Forward limit: (100 / 50) × 9 = **18%**
Aft Limit: (100 / 50) × 29 = **58%**

EASA STUDY GUIDES

MASS & BALANCE

Mass and Balance Self Assessment Test 04 ANSWERS

5	D
6	B
7	D
8	A
9	C
10	B
11	D
12	A

CHAPTER 5
Practical Methods of Calculating Payload

It is often required to calculate specific masses such as the Maximum Take-off Mass (MTOM), the Zero Fuel Mass (MZFM), the Maximum Landing Mass (MLM), the Traffic Load (TL), and / or the fuel.

Maximum Take Off Mass (MTOM) is related to DOM, traffic load and usable fuel as follows:

> MTOM = Dry Operating Mass (DOM) + Traffic Load (TL) + Usable Fuel (UF)

The DOM is the total mass of the aeroplane ready for a specific type of operation excluding all usable fuel and traffic load. The mass includes items such as crew and crew baggage, catering and removable passenger service equipment, portable water and lavatory chemicals, food and beverages.

The Traffic Load is the total mass of passengers, baggage, and cargo, including any non-revenue load.

The Usable Fuel is the total mass of fuel on board the aircraft when it is lined up on the runway.

The MTOM equation may be rearranged to find out any one of the parameters:

> MTOM = DOM + TL + UF
> UF   = MTOM − (DOM + TL)
> TL   = MTOM − (DOM + UF)
> DOM = MTOM − (TL + UF)

There are also two other formulae, which can be used to find out other maximum masses:

> MZFM = DOM + Max TL
> MLM = DOM + Max TL + Reserve Fuel

NOTE: Reserve fuel is the fuel remaining on the aircraft after a flight has been completed.

Another method that may be used to calculate any one of these parameters is by using a load and trim sheet. An example may be found in CAP 696. This may look complicated to use but once mastered will save you a great deal of time in the examination.

> It is not a requirement for CPL students to know how to use the load and trim sheet, however we recommend you learn how to use it as it will save a great deal of time in the examination

If a question provides all three maximum masses, the individual calculations for all three need to be achieved and the lowest (limiting mass) answer is taken. Using the lowest answer ensure that the take-off mass, landing mass, or zero fuel mass is not exceeded.

EASA STUDY GUIDES
MASS & BALANCE

Example 1

Question:
The take-off mass of an aeroplane is 117000 kg, comprising a traffic load of 18000 kg and fuel of 46000 kg. What is the dry operating mass?

Answer:
Calculate Take-off mass (TOM):

Take-off mass (TOM) = Dry operating mass (DOM) + Traffic load (TL) + fuel (UF)

Now place the numbers in the relevant area from the question:

117000 kg (TOM) = DOM + 18000 kg (TL) + 46000 kg (UF)

Now rearrange the equation to calculate the dry operating mass (DOM):

DOM = 117000 kg – 18000 kg – 46000 kg

DOM = 53000 kg

Example 2

Question:
The dry operating mass of an aircraft is 2000 kg. The maximum take-off mass, landing and zero fuel mass are identical at 3500 kg. The block fuel mass is 550 kg, and the taxi fuel mass is 50 kg. The available mass of payload is:

Answer
Use the same principle as in Example 1 but this time for all three maximum masses given in this question:

When calculating take-off fuel, taxi fuel must be substituted from block fuel. Therefore 550 kg – 50 kg = 500 kg take off fuel

3500 kg (MTOM) = 2000 kg (DOM) + TL + 500 kg (UF)
    TL = 3500 kg – 2000 kg – 500 kg
    TL = 1000 kg

3500 kg (MZFM) = 2000 kg (DOM) + TL
    TL = 3500 kg – 2000 kg
    TL = 1500 kg

Maximum landing mass cannot be calculated since trip fuel or a fuel consumption rate has not been given.

5.1 Useful load

Useful load may be thought of as things that are useful for the flight (i.e. fuel / passengers and / or freight). A formula, which relates to this is:

Useful Load = TOM – DOM

Example:
If the Basic Empty mass is 61300 kg. The mass of operational items (including crew) is 2300 kg. TOM is 132000 kg (including useable fuel quantity of 43800 kg) the useful load is: 68400 kg.

DOM = BEM + CREW
DOM = 61300 kg + 2300 kg
DOM = 63600 kg

Using the Useful Load formula:

Useful Load = TOM – DOM
Useful Load = 132000 kg – 63600 kg
Useful Load = 68400 kg

EASA STUDY GUIDES

MASS & BALANCE

CIVIL AVIATION AUTHORITY
MASS & BALANCE

DATA SHEET
MRJT 1

Figure 4.14 Load and Trim Sheet (Blank)

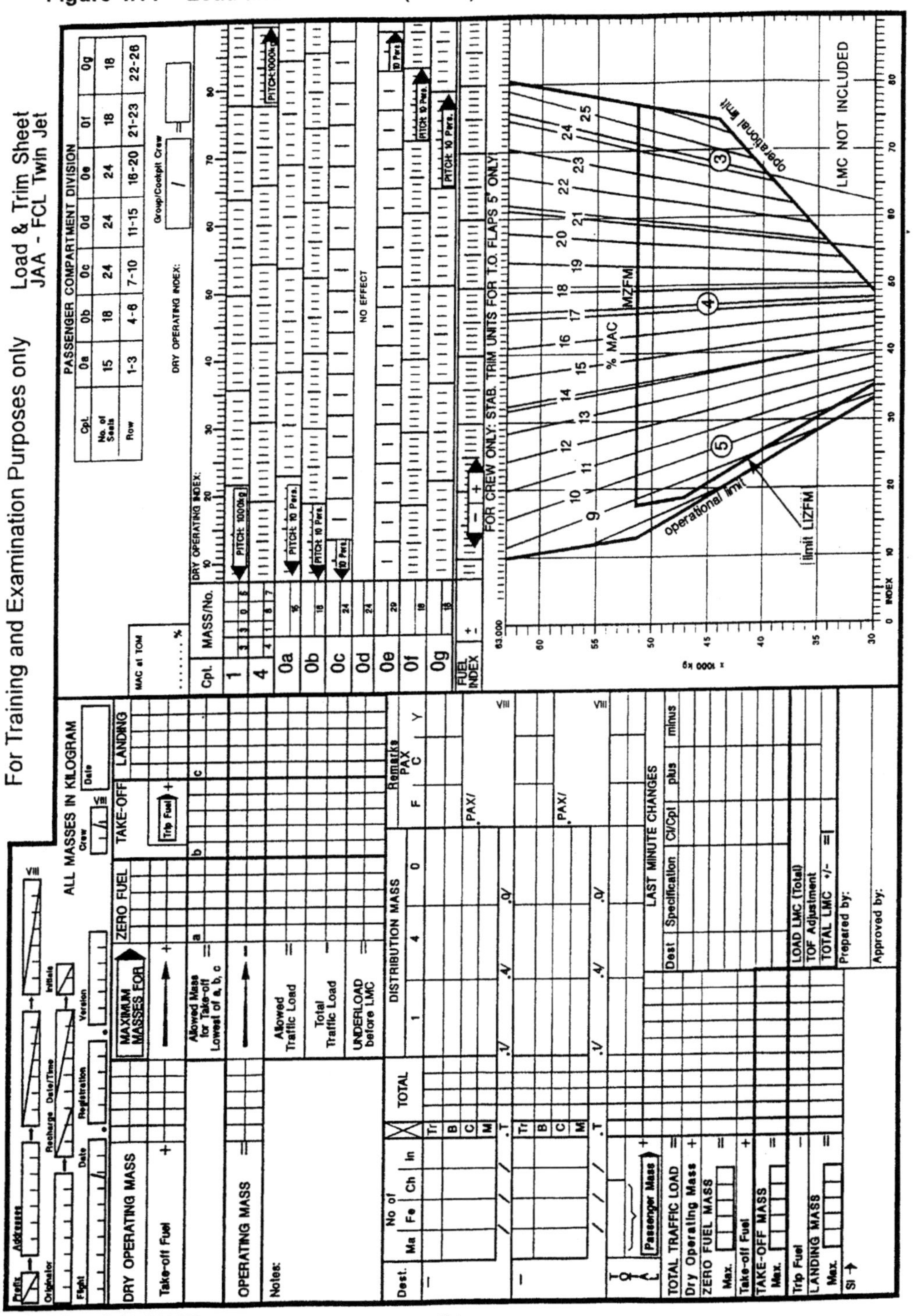

Figure 5.1 Load and trim sheet (blank)

EASA STUDY GUIDES

MASS & BALANCE

5.2 Using the Load and Trim Sheet

The load and trim sheet (as shown in the example at Figure 4.12 CAP 696) is in two parts.

Part A (on the left) is a loading summary, which is completed as follows:

Section 1: Used to establish the limiting take-off mass; maximum allowable traffic load; under-load before last minute changes (LMC).

Section 2: Shows the distribution of the traffic load.
In this section the following abbreviations are used:
- TR — Transit
- B — Baggage
- C — Cargo
- M — Mail
- Pax — Passengers
- Pax F — First Class
- Pax C — Club / Business
- Pax M — Economy

Section 3: Used to summarise load and cross check that limits have not been exceeded.

The example shown uses the following data:

DOM	34300 kg	Passengers	130 (average mass 84 kg)
MZFM	51300 kg	Baggage	130 (14 kg per piece)
DOI	45.0	Cargo	630 kg
MTOM	62800 kg	Fuel Total	14500 kg
MLM	54900 kg	Flight Fuel	8500 kg

DOI: Dry Operating Index (position of the centre of gravity at the aircrafts Dry Operating Mass)

Index = Moment ÷ Constant

EASA STUDY GUIDES

MASS & BALANCE

The loading summary is completed as follows:

1. Enter the basic data given in the example. DOM is 34300 kg, Maximum masses for zero fuel are 51300 kg and landing are 54900 kg.

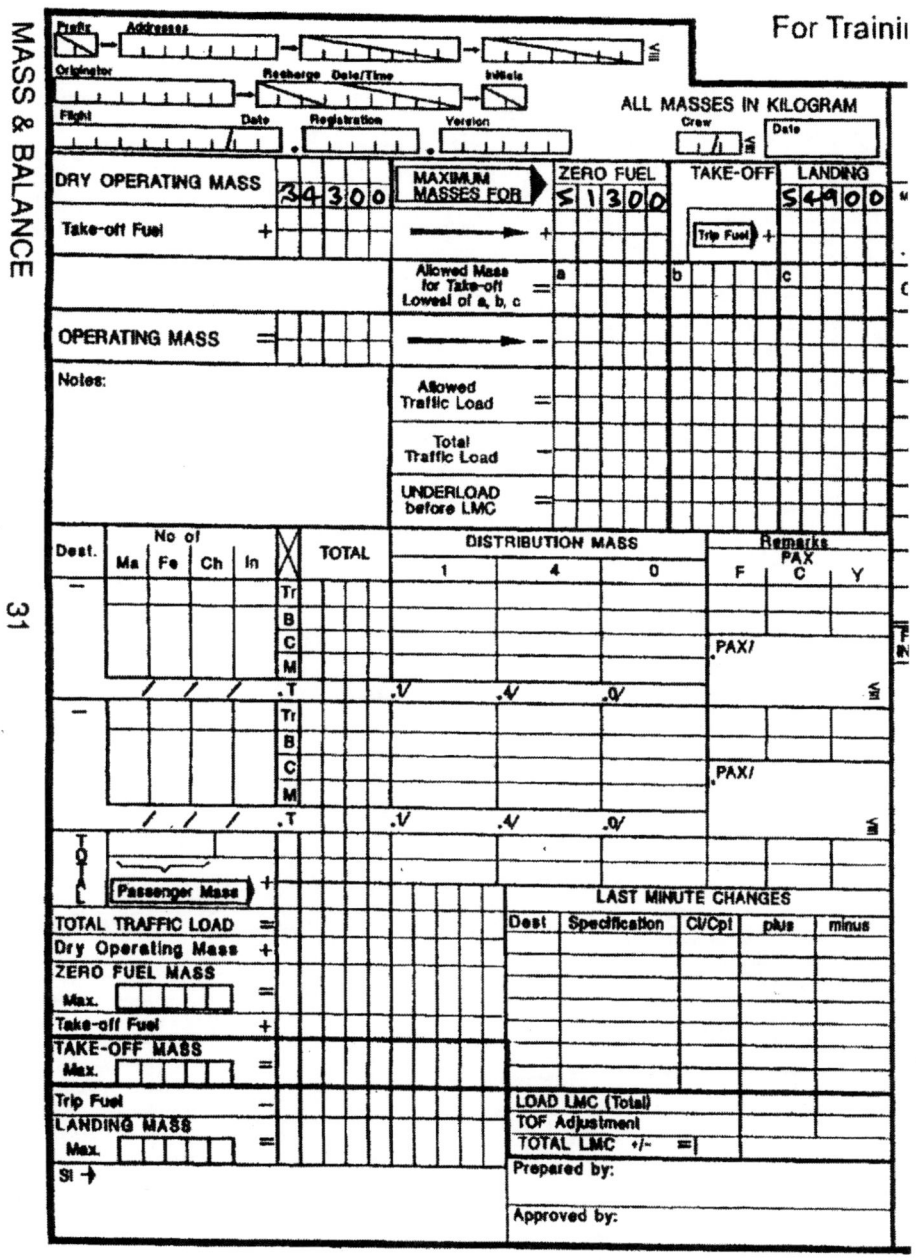

Figure 5.2 Entering the basic data

2   Enter fuel, but remember to put in take off fuel and not block fuel. In order to calculate take off fuel you must minus taxi fuel from your block fuel. Take-off fuel is 14500 kg. An arrow to the right of this indicates that this value should be transferred over to the zero fuel column. Write in the trip fuel under the landing mass column where it specifies "trip fuel".

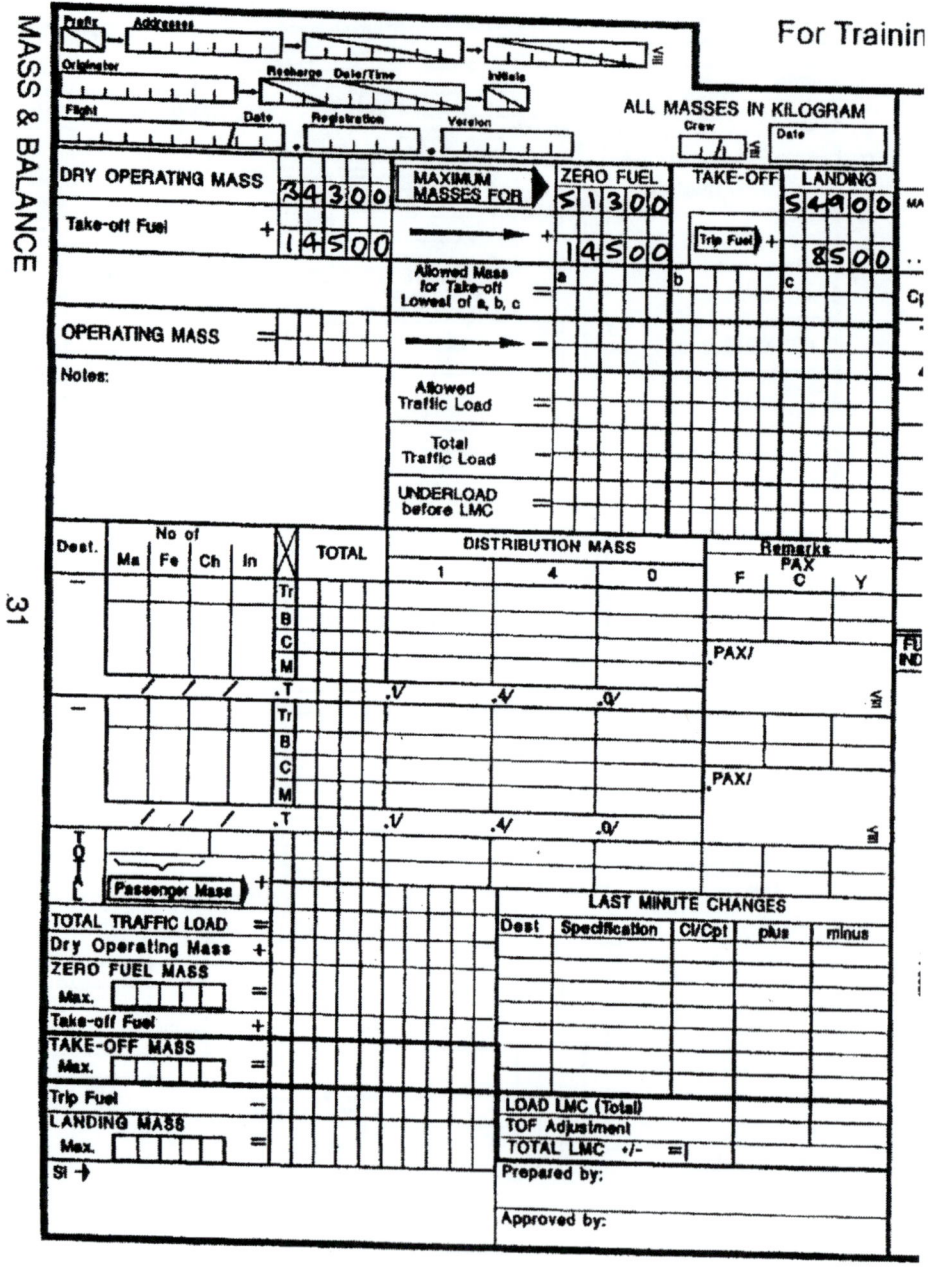

Figure 5.3 Enter the fuel

3   Follow the instructions on the trim sheet and add the values up and write the values in the correct rows and column.

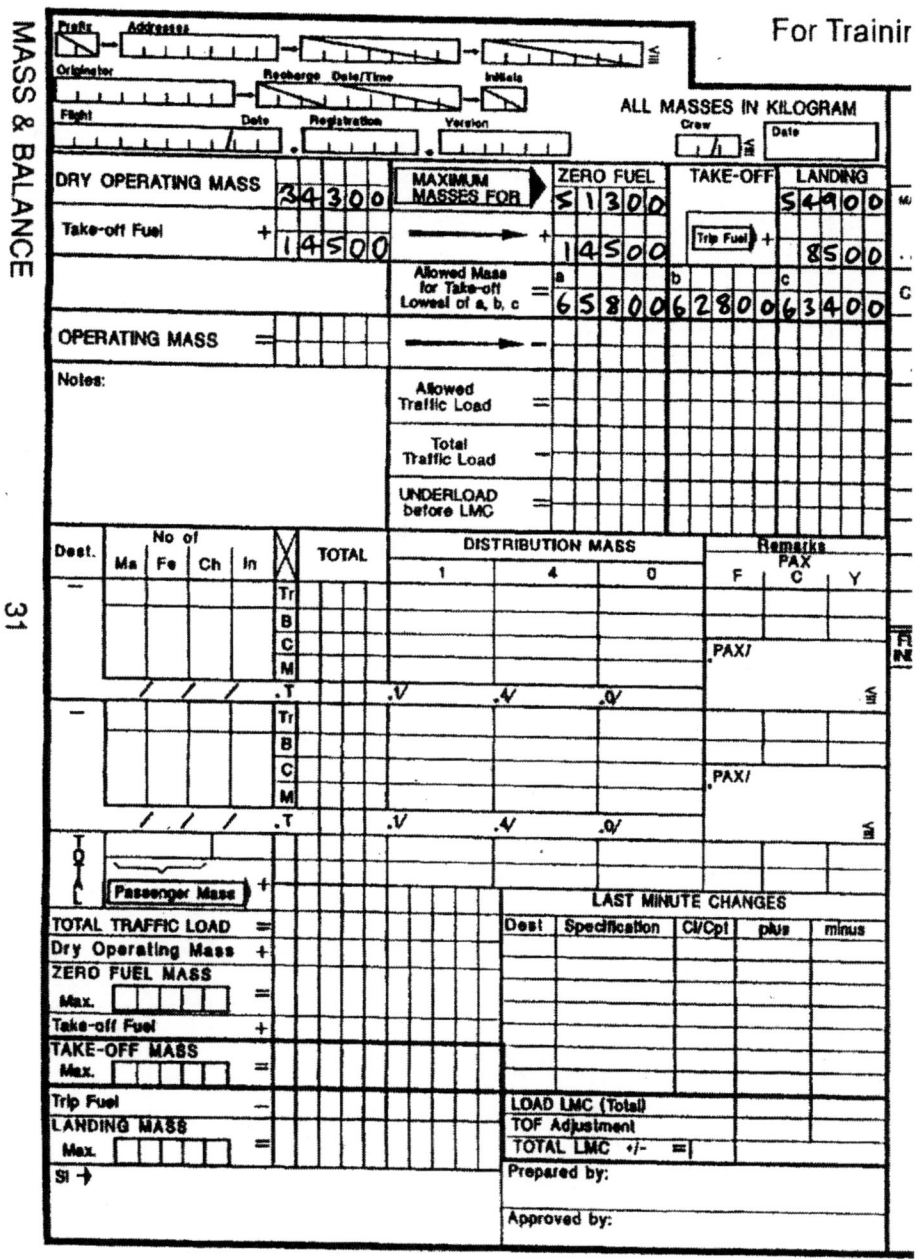

Figure 5.4 follow the instructions on the trim sheet

4   Select the lowest mass from column A, B and C. (Calculate the operating mass on the left and enter this under the lowest mass).

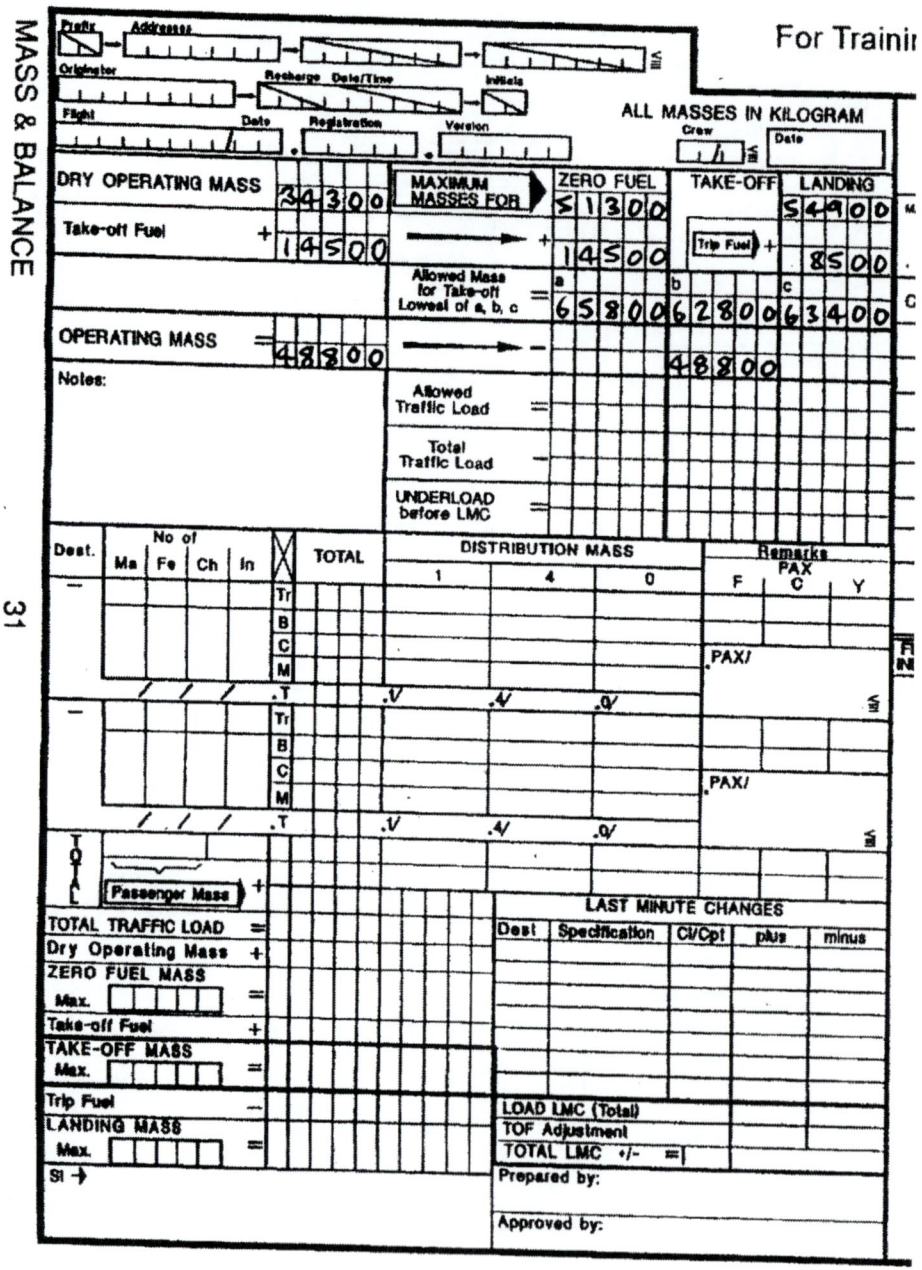

Figure 5.5 Selecting the lowest mass

5   Follow the instructions on the table and subtract the operating mass from the lowest value. This provides the traffic load. Repeat the process following the instructions to calculate the total traffic load and underload:

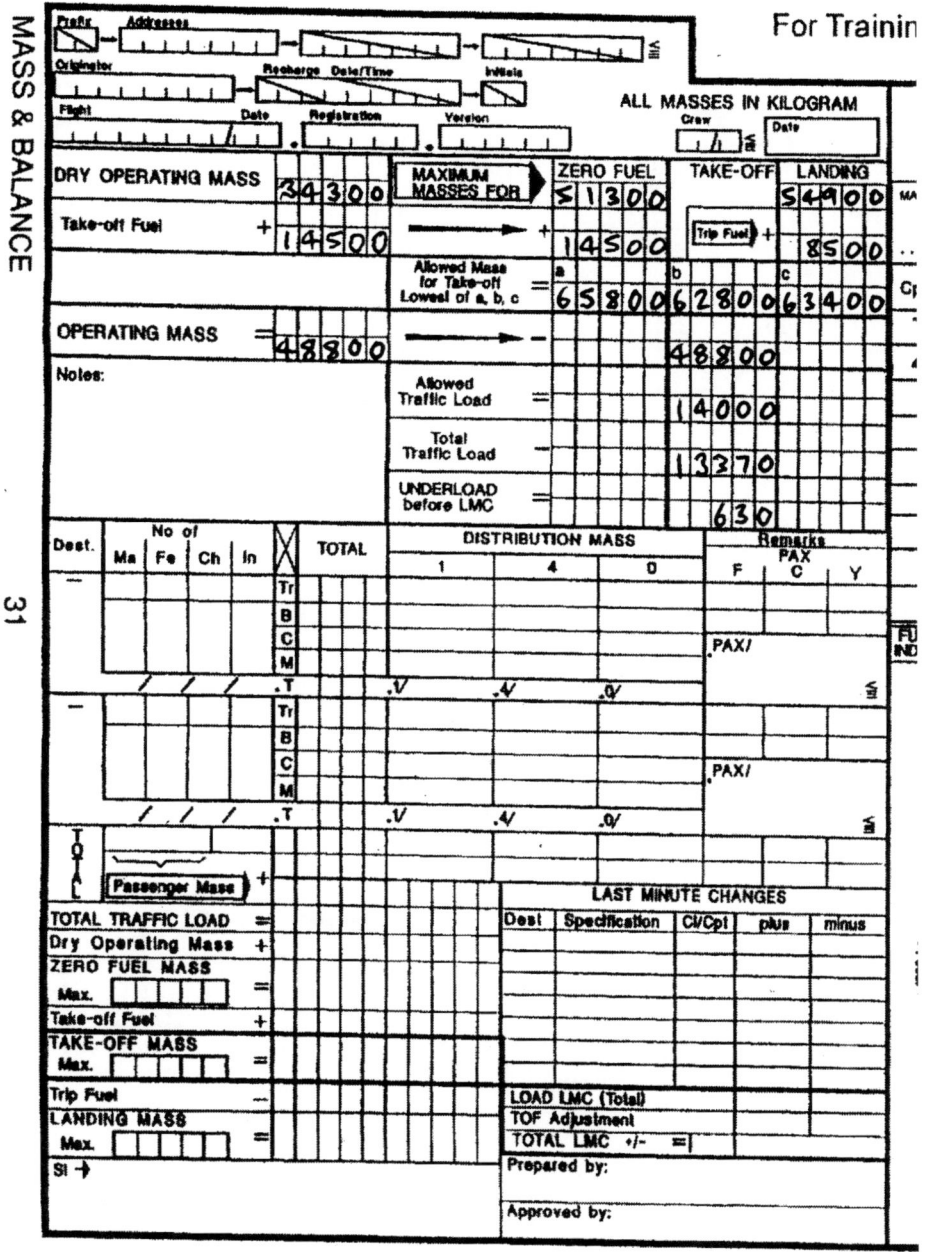

Figure 5.6 calculating traffic load and underload

6   Destination (in this case LMG is the abbreviation for Limoges) and traffic load Distribution are usually given:

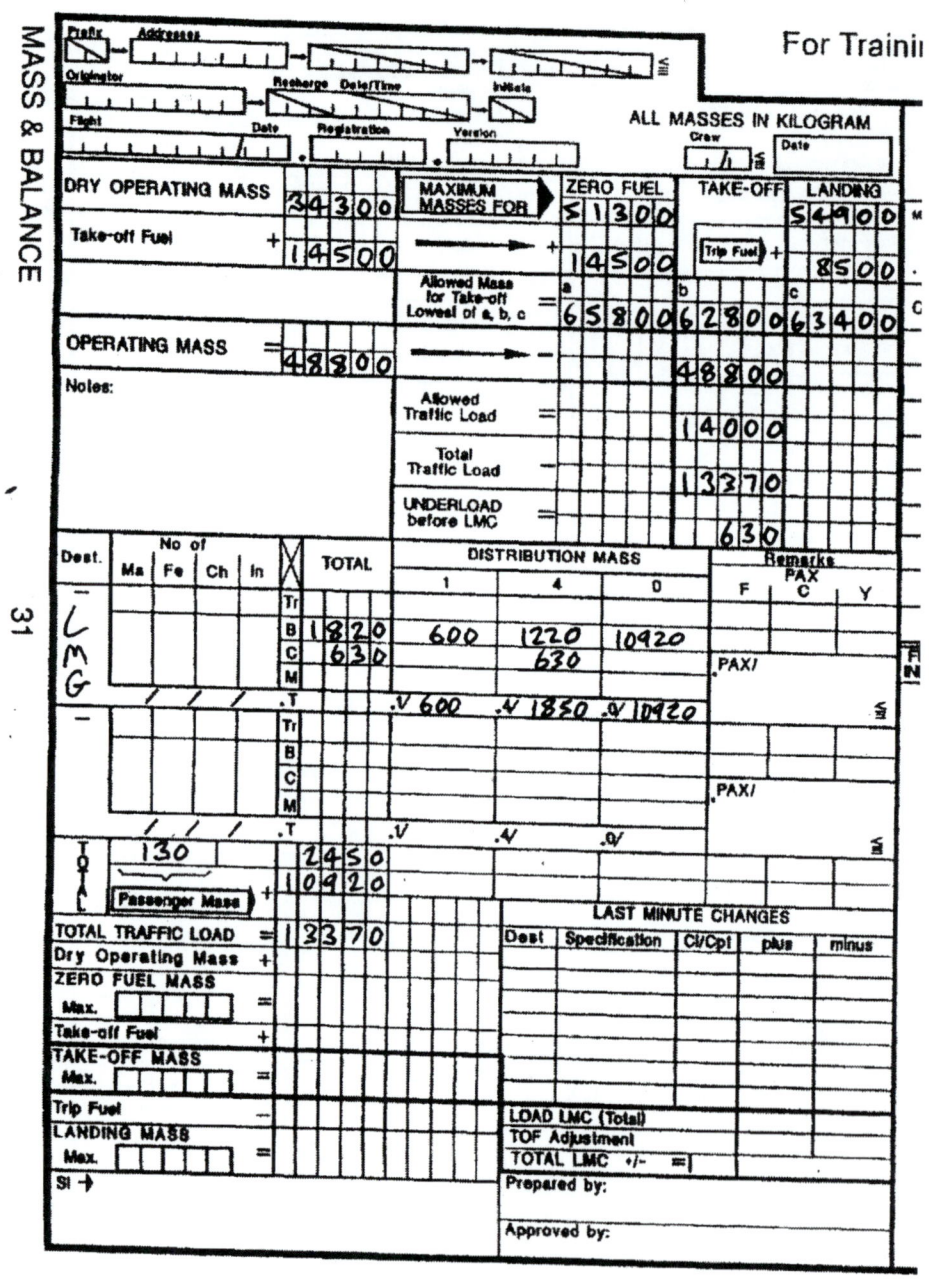

Figure 5.7 Destination and traffic load distribution

EASA STUDY GUIDES
MASS & BALANCE

7   Calculate (cross check) Zero Fuel Mass, Take Off Mass, and Landing Mass:

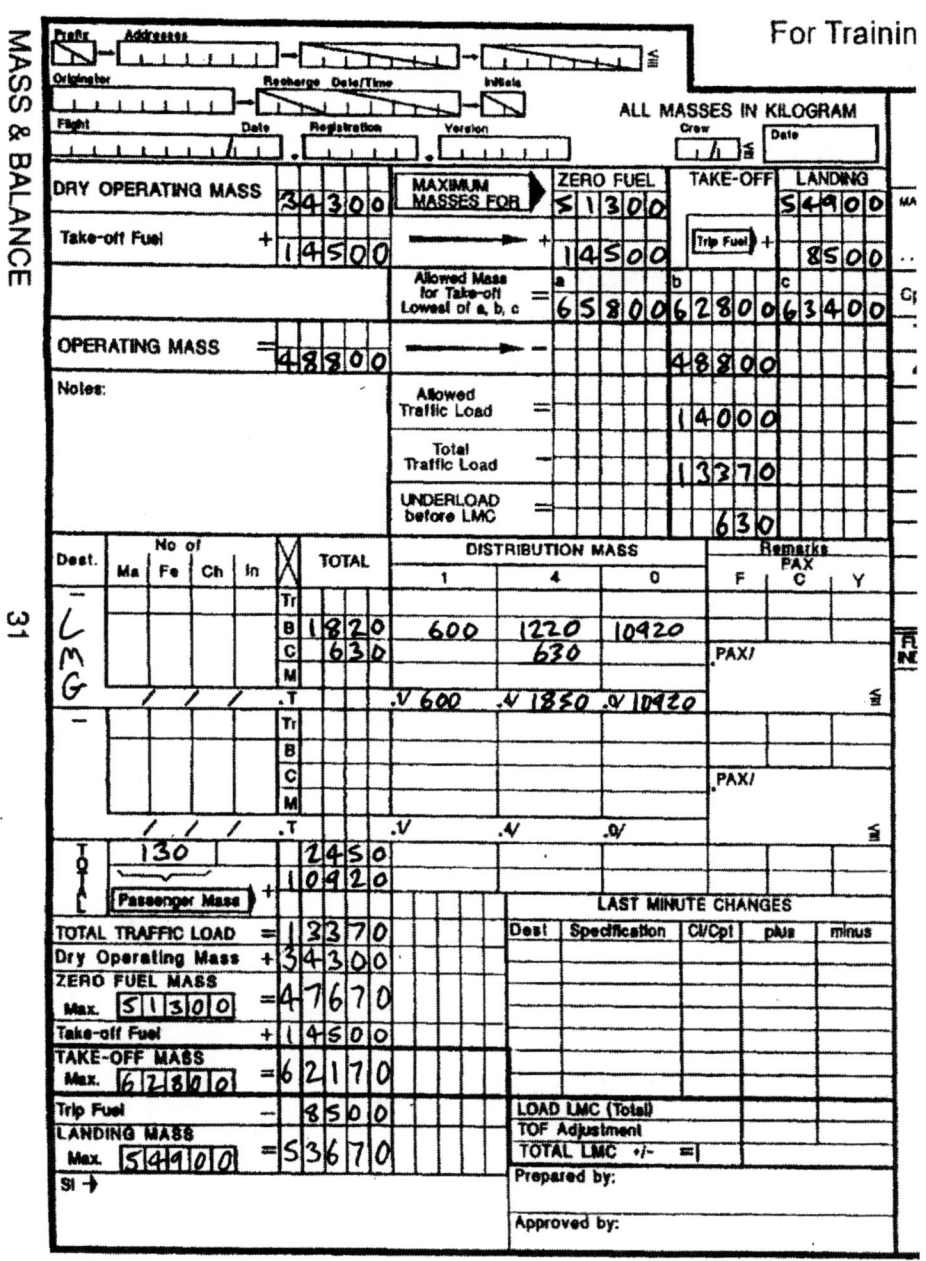

Figure 5.8 Cross checking ZFM, TOM and LM

EASA STUDY GUIDES

MASS & BALANCE

8   Enter the last minute changes (LMC) if any, for example 1 male passenger travelling to LMG in compartment 0a weighing 84 kg:

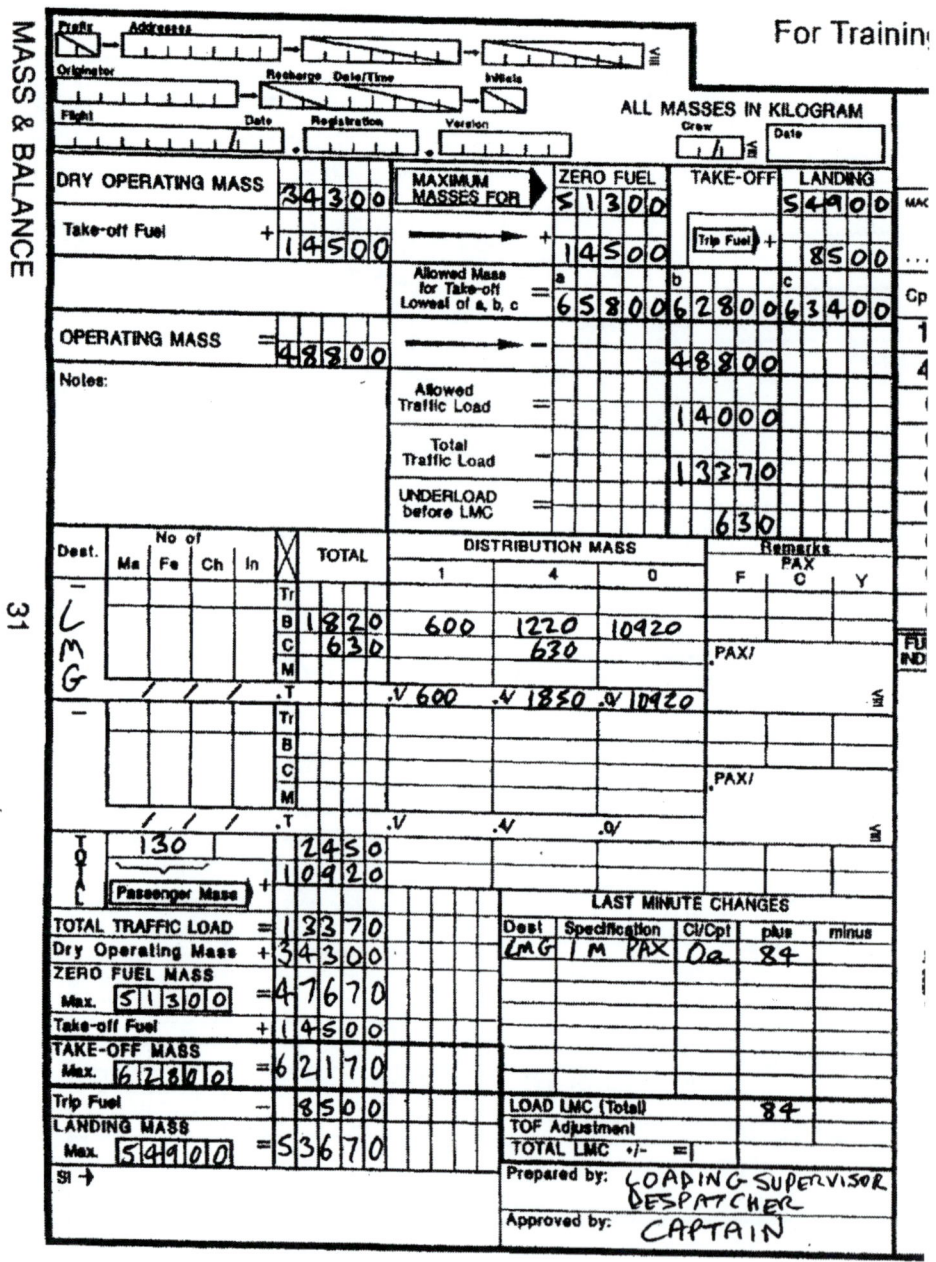

Figure 5.9 Entering last minute changes

Part B (on the right) is the trim sheet, which is completed as follows:

1. Using data from the loading summary, start by entering the index for the DOM.
2. Move the index in turn (for the mass in each cargo hold) then in accordance with the passenger distribution.
3. Establish the CG % MAC at ZFM and ensure that it lies within the envelope.
4. Add the fuel index correction to obtain the TOM index and ensure that the CG lies within the envelope. Extract the % MAC value for the TOM / CG position.

Start by entering the Index.

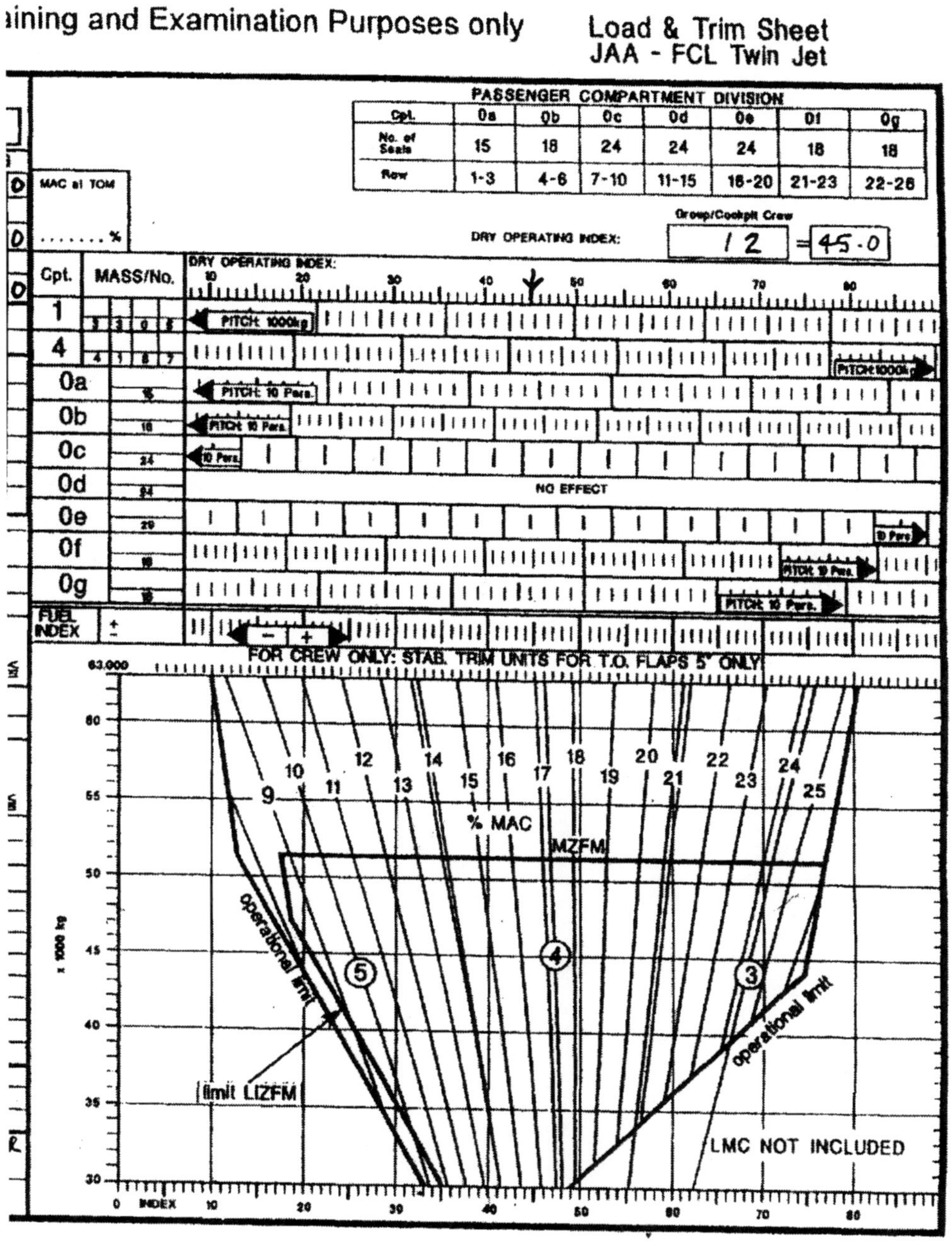

Figure 5.10 Entering the DOI

9   Following the values on the left hand side, position the line as indicated by the horizontal pitch arrows and continue the same process until the bottom of the table is reached:

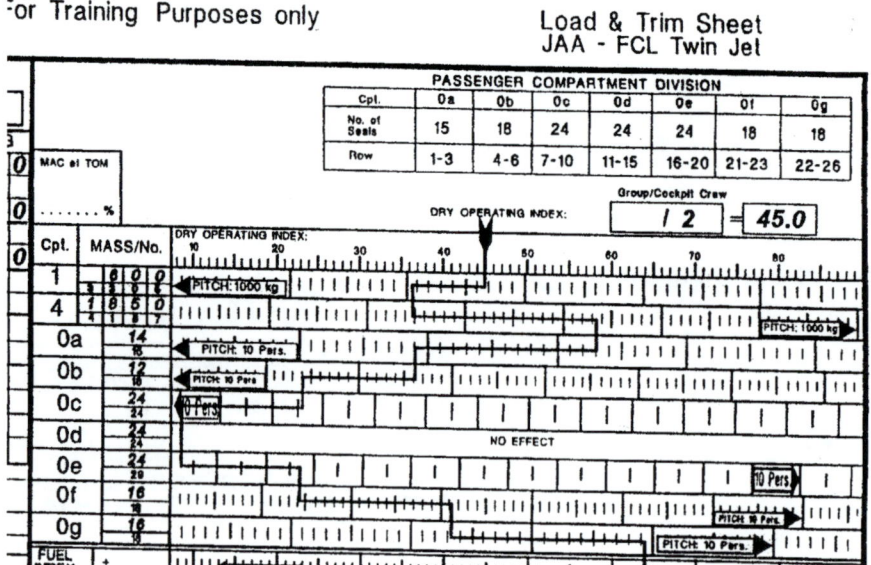

Figure 5.11 Adjusting the CG

As you leave compartment 0g, your aircraft is at zero fuel mass. You now need to add Take-Off fuel of 14,500 kg. The index unit, which corresponds to this mass, may be found in CAP 696 Figure 4.13 (Fuel index correction table). For fuel mass figures not printed in this table the index of the next higher mass is applicable (e.g. 14500 kg is not found in the table so use the next higher mass of 14580 kg which corresponds to an index unit of –12.9).

CIVIL AVIATION AUTHORITY
MASS & BALANCE

DATA SHEET
MRJT 1

Figure 4.13   FUEL INDEX CORRECTION TABLE

	Fuel Mass (Kg)	Index Units	Fuel Mass (Kg)	Index Units
	500	-1.0	9330	-0.3
	750	-1.5	9580	-0.9
	1000	-1.9	9830	-1.5
	1250	-2.3	10080	-2.1
	1500	-2.6	10330	-2.7
	1750	-3.0	10580	-3.3
	2000	-3.3	10830	-3.9
	2500	-3.7	11080	-4.5
	3000	-4.3	11330	-5.1
	3500	-4.7	11580	-5.7
	4000	-5.1	11830	-6.3
	4500	-5.4	12080	-6.9
	5000	-5.7	12330	-7.5
	5500	-5.9	12580	-8.1
	6000	-6.0	12830	-8.7
	6500	-6.1	13080	-9.3
	7000	-5.9	13330	-9.9
	7500	-5.0	13580	-10.5
	7670	-4.6	13830	-11.1
	7830	-4.1	14080	-11.7
	8000	-3.7	14330	-12.3
	8170	-3.2	14580	-12.9
	8330	-2.6	14830	-13.5
	8500	-2.1	15080	-14.1
	8630	-1.6	15330	-14.8
	8750	-1.1	15580	-15.4
	8880	-0.6	15830	-16.3
	9000	-0.1	16080	-17.1
tanks 1 & 2 full	9080	+0.3	centre tank full 16140	-17.3

Useable fuel quantities in lines = 20 Kg. (included in the tables).
Interpolation not necessary!

For mass figures not printed in these tables the index of the next higher mass is applicable.

Figure 5.12 Fuel index correction table

10 The fuel index value of −12.9 may be used in the fuel index row as indicated by the horizontal arrows.

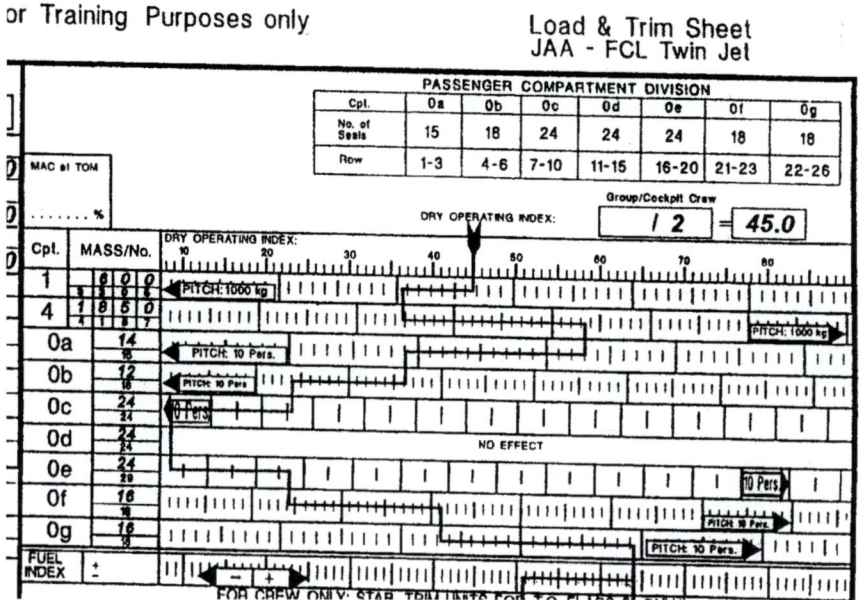

Figure 5.13 Fuel index row

11 You now have two lines, which you can drop down to the actual Take Off Mass (TOM) which includes the take-off fuel, and the actual Zero Fuel Mass (ZFM). By looking at the ZFM you can see that the MAC is 22.5%, and TOM is 18.3%.

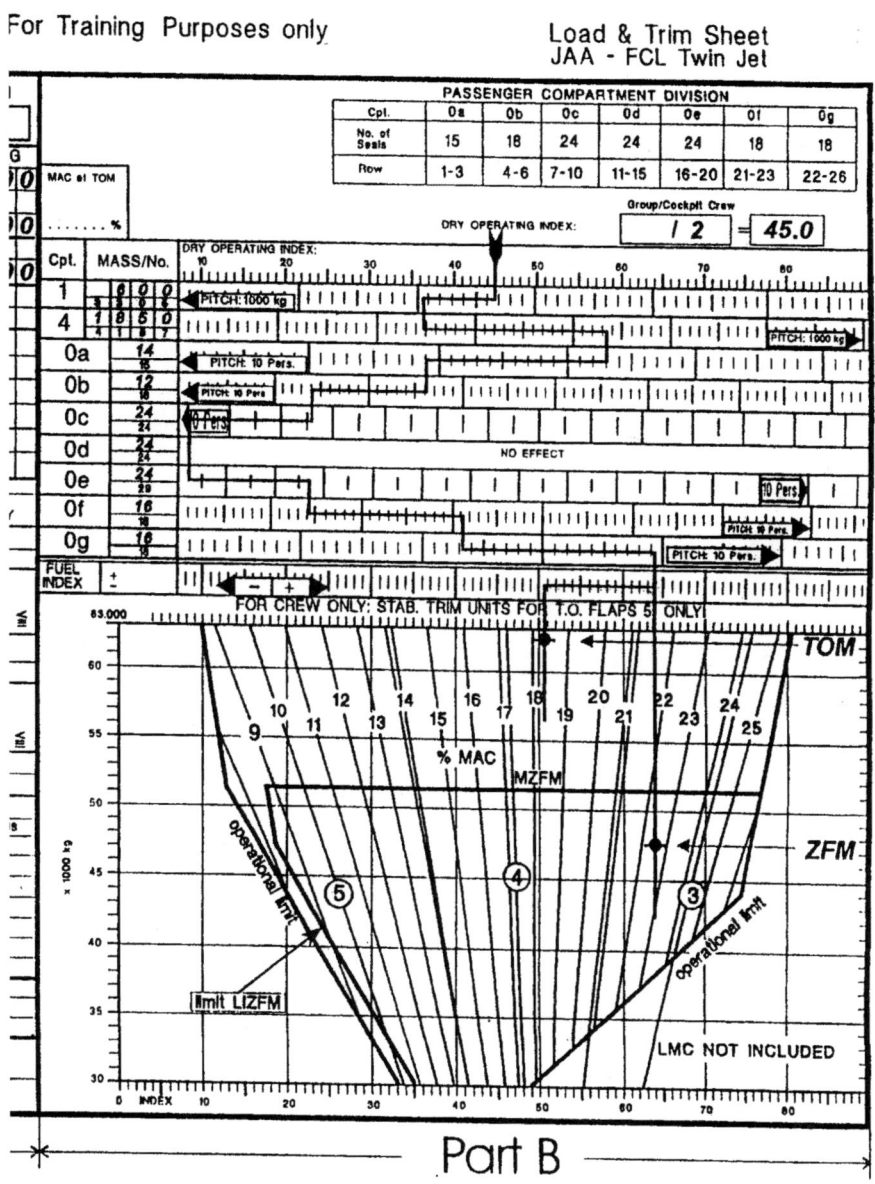

Figure 5.14 Calculating MAC

EASA STUDY GUIDES

MASS & BALANCE

For the following example use both the equation method and the load and trim sheet to illustrate that both methods come out with the same answer.

Example 1:
Given: Dry operating mass = 29800 kg Maximum take-off mass = 52400 kg Maximum zero-fuel mass = 43100 kg Maximum landing mass = 46700 kg Trip Fuel = 4000 kg Fuel quantity at brake release = 8000 kg What is the maximum traffic load?
Using the equation method: 52400 kg (MTOM) = 29800 kg (DOM) + TL + 8000 kg (UF) ⟶ TL = 14600 kg 43100 kg (MZFM) = 29800 kg (DOM) + TL ⟶ TL = 13300 kg 46700 kg (MLM) = 29800 kg (DOM) + TL + 4000 kg (UF) ⟶ TL = **12900 kg** Having calculated the traffic load for all three maximum masses choose the lowest value as the maximum traffic load that can be used on the aircraft, of 12900 kg.

Now use the load and trim sheet method with reference to the previous pages to work out the same value. After practice the load and trim sheet can save a great deal of time

EASA STUDY GUIDES

MASS & BALANCE

Mass and Balance Self Assessment Test 05

1. Determine the actual take-off mass from the following :
   - Maximum structural take-off mass   48000 kg
   - Maximum structural landing mass: 44000 kg
   - Maximum zero fuel mass: 36000 kg
   -Taxi fuel: 600 kg
   -Contingency fuel: 900 kg
   -Alternate fuel: 800 kg
   -Final reserve fuel: 1100 kg
   -Trip fuel: 9000 kg
   A) 48 400 kg
   B) 53 000 kg
   C) 47 800 kg
   D) 48 000 kg

2. Given:
   Dry Operating Mass=   29800 kg
   Maximum Take-Off Mass=   52400 kg
   Maximum Zero-Fuel Mass=   43100 kg
   Maximum Landing Mass=   46700 kg
   Trip fuel=   4000 kg
   Fuel quantity at brakes release=   8000 kg
   The maximum traffic load is:
   A) 12900 kg
   B) 13300 kg
   C) 9300 kg
   D) 14600 kg

3. The take-off mass of an aeroplane is 117 000 kg, comprising a traffic load of 18 000 kg and fuel of 46 000 kg. What is the dry operating mass?
   A) 71 000 kg
   B) 99 000 kg
   C) 53 000 kg
   D) 64 000 kg

4. The DOM of an aircraft is 2000 kg. The MTOM, LM and ZFM are identical at 3500 kg. The block fuel mass is 550kg, and the taxi fuel mass is 50 kg. The available mass of payload is:
   A) 1450 kg
   B) 1000 kg
   C) 950 kg
   D) 1500 kg

5. Given an aeroplane with:
   Maximum Structural Landing Mass: 68000 kg
   ım Zero Fuel Mass: 70200 kg
   ım Structural Take-off Mass: 78200 kg
   ərating Mass :   48000 kg
   led trip fuel is 7000 kg and the reserve fuel is 2800 kg

   Assuming performance limitations are not restricting, the maximum permitted take-off mass and maximum traffic load are respectively:
   A) 75000 kg and 20000 kg
   B) 77200 kg and 19400 kg
   C) 77200 kg and 22200 kg
   D) 75000 kg and 17200 kg

CRANFIELD AVIATION TRAINING SCHOOL LTD. PART-FCL ATO N° 276
CATS INNOVATION CENTRE, LUTON, Bedfordshire LU2 8DL U.K.

www.catsaviation.com

Mass & Balance

6   (For this question refer to CAP696 MRJT 1 Figure 4.14)
    A revenue flight is planned for the transport aeroplane. Take-off mass is not airfield limited. The following data applies:

Dry Operating Mass	34930 kg
Performance limited landing mass	55000 kg
Fuel on board at ramp-	
Taxi fuel	350 kg
Trip fuel	9730 kg
Contingency and final reserve fuel	1200 kg
Alternate fuel	1600 kg
Passengers on board	130
Standard mass for each passenger	84 kg
Baggage per passenger	14 kg
Traffic load	Maximum possible

    Use the loading manual provided and the above data. Determine the maximum cargo load that may be carried without exceeding the limiting aeroplane landing mass.

A) 5400 kg
B) 6350 kg.
C) 3185 kg.
D) 4530 kg.

7   TOM is 302550 kg. Take-off fuel on board (including contingency and alternate of 19450 kg) is 121450 kg. The DOM is 161450 kg. What is the useful load?

A   181100 kg
B   19650 kg
C   141100 kg
D   1411000 kg

EASA STUDY GUIDES

MASS & BALANCE

Mass and Balance Self Assessment Test 05 ANSWERS

1	C
2	A
3	C
4	B
5	D
6	D
7	C

CHAPTER 6
Floor Loading

The distribution of weight of a box is dependent on the surface area that is in contact with the ground. If a larger area is placed on the floor of the cargo bay then the load will have a larger distribution, lessening the load (force) acting on a point per unit area.

6.1 Distribution Load:

Distribution load is the load that is exerted (or distributed) as a force over a unit area. A box of different dimensions will distribute its weight according to its surface area. The side of a box with the larger surface area will distribute its weight more than the side with the smaller surface area.

$$\text{Distribution Load (m}^2\text{)} = \text{Mass} \div \text{Area (m}^2\text{)}$$

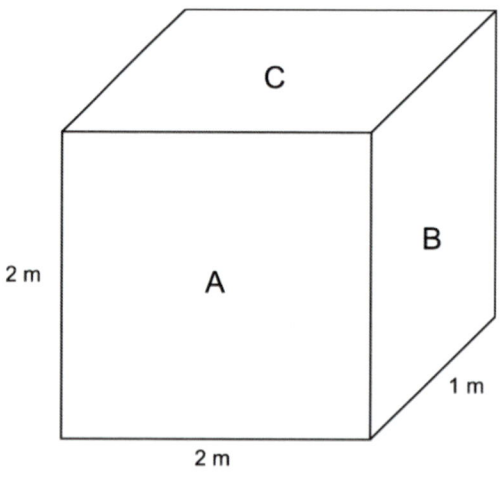

Figure 6.1   2 x 2 x 1 m box

A box of dimensions: height 2 m, width 2 m and depth 1 m has sides of different surface areas. The distribution load will depend upon which side of the box is placed upon the floor. If the box has a total mass of 500 kg the load exerted on the floor may be either 125 kg / m^2 or 250 kg / m^2, depending on which side is placed on the floor.   Area = Width x Height, therefore:

Side	Area			Distribution Load
Side A =	2 x 2	=	4 m^2	125 kg / m^2
Side B =	2 x 1	=	2 m^2	250 kg / m^2
Side C =	2 x 1	=	2 m^2	250 kg / m^2

If the distribution load limit was 240 kg / m^2 then this box could not be placed in a cargo hold on side B or side C but could be placed on side A (the side with a calculated distribution load less than the limit.

EASA STUDY GUIDES

MASS & BALANCE

6.2 Running Load:

Running load is the weight per unit length. It represents the amount of weight that can be placed onto an aircraft runner without breaking it. Running load is measured in metres and not metres squared as it is a load per unit length.

Running Load (m) = Mass ÷ Length (m)	
Mass ÷ Length	Running Load
= 500 ÷ 2	250 kg / m
= 500 ÷ 2	250 kg / m
= 500 ÷ 1	500 kg / m

Example 1

Question:

Example:
The maximum load per running metre of an aeroplane is 350 kg / m. The width of the floor area is 2 m. The floor strength limitation is 300 kg / m^2. Which one of the following crates (length x width x height) can be loaded directly on the floor?

   A load of 400 kg in a crate with dimensions 1.2 m x 1.2 m x 1.2 m
   A load of 500 kg in a crate with dimensions 1.5 m x 1 m x 1 m
   A load of 400 kg in a crate with dimensions 1.4 m x 0.8 m x 0.8 m
   A load of 700 kg in a crate with dimensions 1.8 m x 1.4 m x 0.8 m

Solution:
First of all the distribution and running loads need to be defined. In order to find these the units need to be looked at. The distribution load is a weight per unit area and is measured in kg / m^2, therefore look for a value with those units, i.e. 300 kg / m^2. The maximum running load is 350 kg / m as it is a weight per unit length.

Don't forget to read the question. It states that the width of the floor is 2 m; therefore if any of the lengths were greater than 2 m then it wouldn't fit into the cargo hold and couldn't be used. The most favourable way to approach a question like this is to work through each answer one-by-one.

Box A

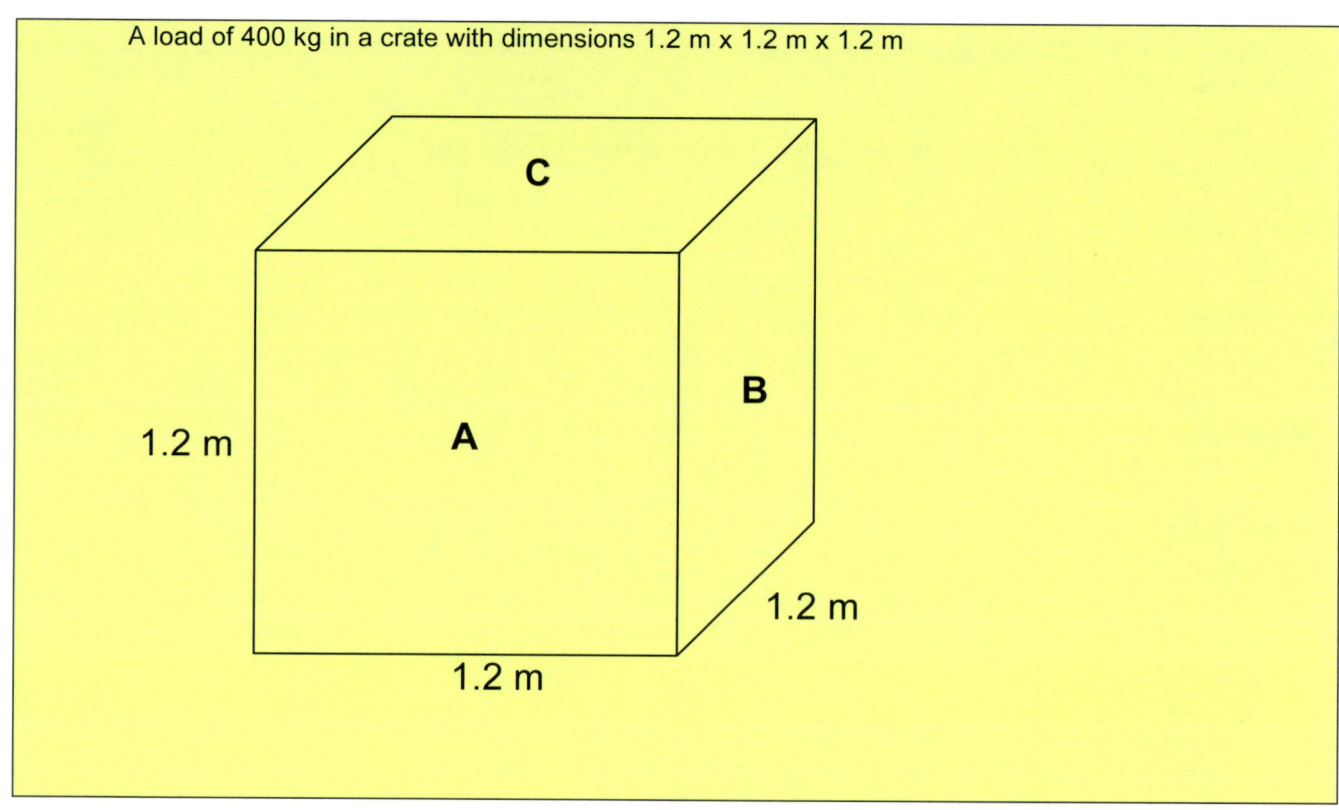

Side			Area	Distribution Load
Side A =	1.2 x 1.2	=	1.44 m²	278 kg / m²
Side B =	1.2 x 1.2	=	1.44 m²	278 kg / m²
Side C =	1.2 x 1.2	=	1.44 m²	278 kg / m²

With reference to the distribution load, the floor strength limitation in the example is 300 kg / m². All of the above values (278 kg / m²) are below 300 kg / m² so the package may be placed on any side. Now the running load needs to be calculated:

Mass ÷ Length			Running Load
= 400	÷	1.2	333 kg / m
= 400	÷	1.2	333 kg / m
= 400	÷	1.2	333 kg / m

With reference to the running load the maximum in the example is 350 kg / m. Once again all of the above values are below 350 kg / m so the package is within the limits of both the distribution and running loads.

Even though answer A is correct the remaining answers must be worked through to certify that there is only one correct answer.

EASA STUDY GUIDES

MASS & BALANCE

Box B

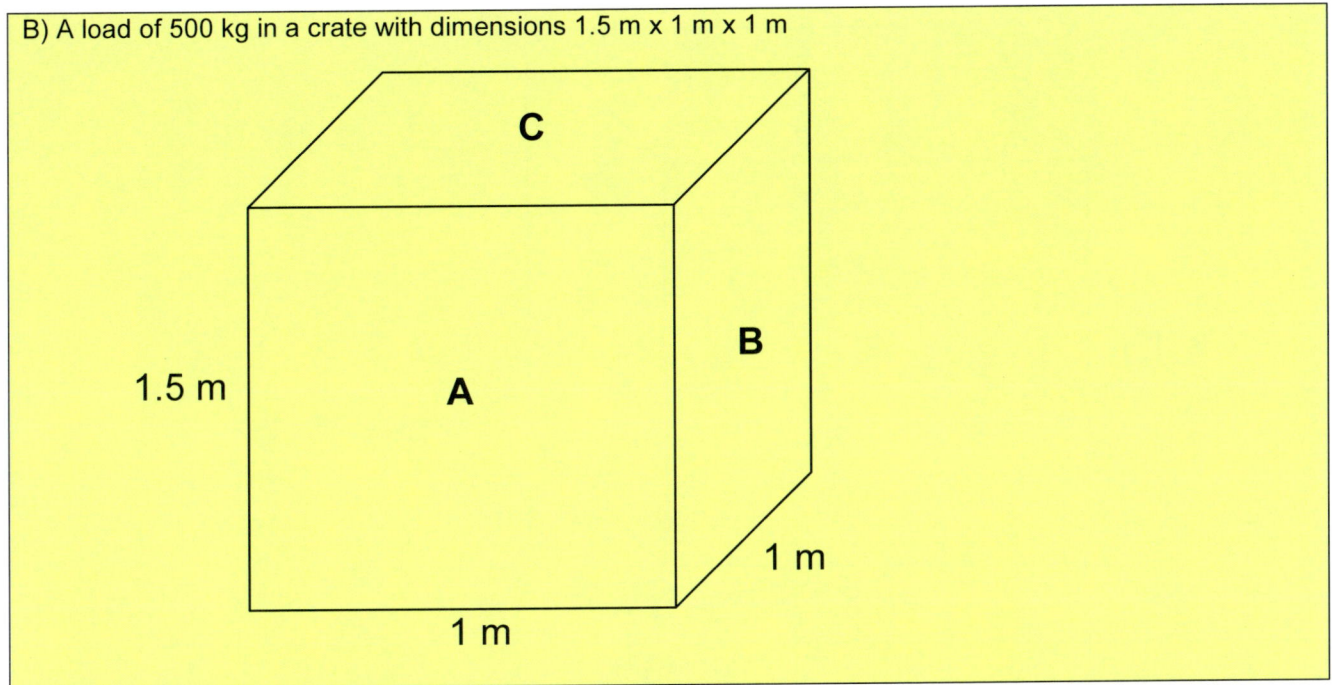

B) A load of 500 kg in a crate with dimensions 1.5 m x 1 m x 1 m

Side	Area	Distribution Load
Side A = 1.5 x 1 = 1.5 m²		333 kg / m²
Side B = 1.5 x 1 = 1.5 m²		333 kg / m²
Side C = 1 x 1 = 1 m²		500 kg / m²

With reference to the distribution load, the maximum is 300 kg / m². All of the values are above 300 kg / m² so immediately it can be seen that the box cannot be placed onto the aircraft as it will exceed the maximum distribution load. There is no need to calculate the running load.

Box C

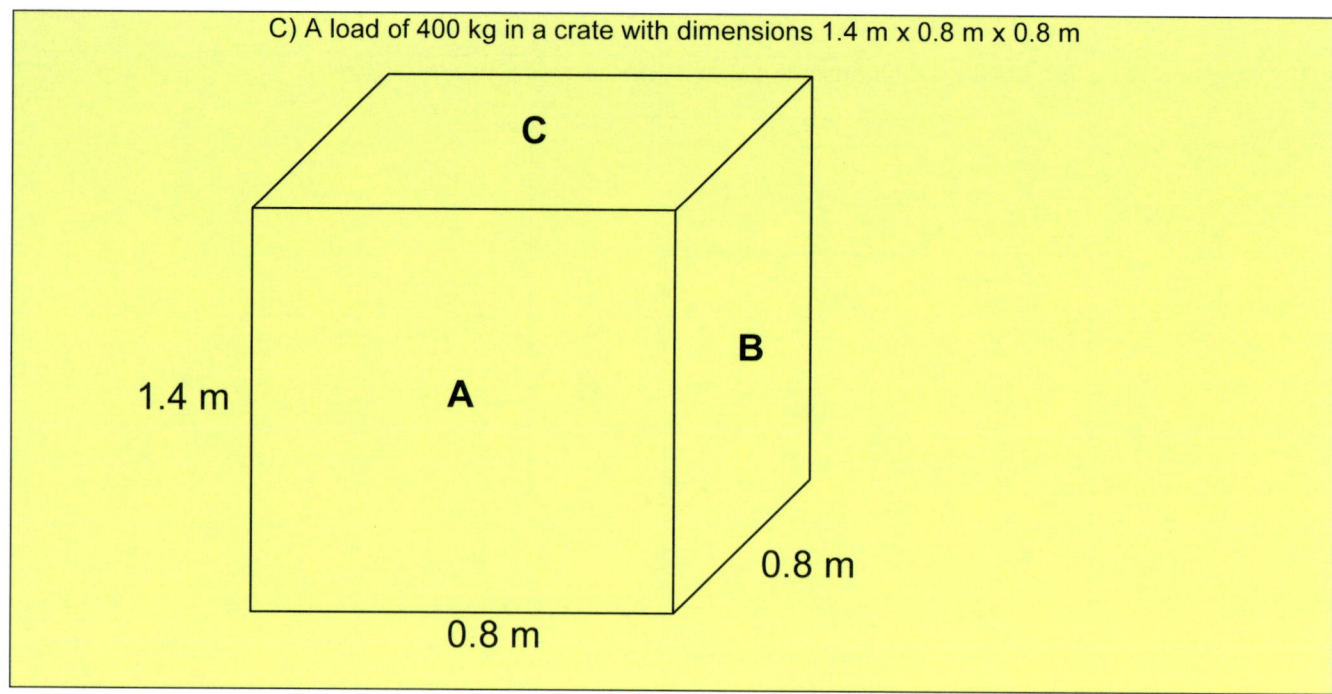

C) A load of 400 kg in a crate with dimensions 1.4 m x 0.8 m x 0.8 m

Side	Area			Distribution Load
Side A =	1.4 x 0.8	=	1.12 m^2	357 kg / m^2
Side B =	1.4 x 0.8	=	1.12 m^2	357 kg / m^2
Side C =	0.8 x 0.8	=	0.64 m^2	625 kg / m^2

With reference to the distribution load, the maximum is 300 kg / m^2. All of the values are above 300 kg / m^2 so immediately it can be seen that the box cannot be placed onto the aircraft as it will exceed the maximum distribution load. There is no need to calculate the running load.

EASA STUDY GUIDES

MASS & BALANCE

Box D

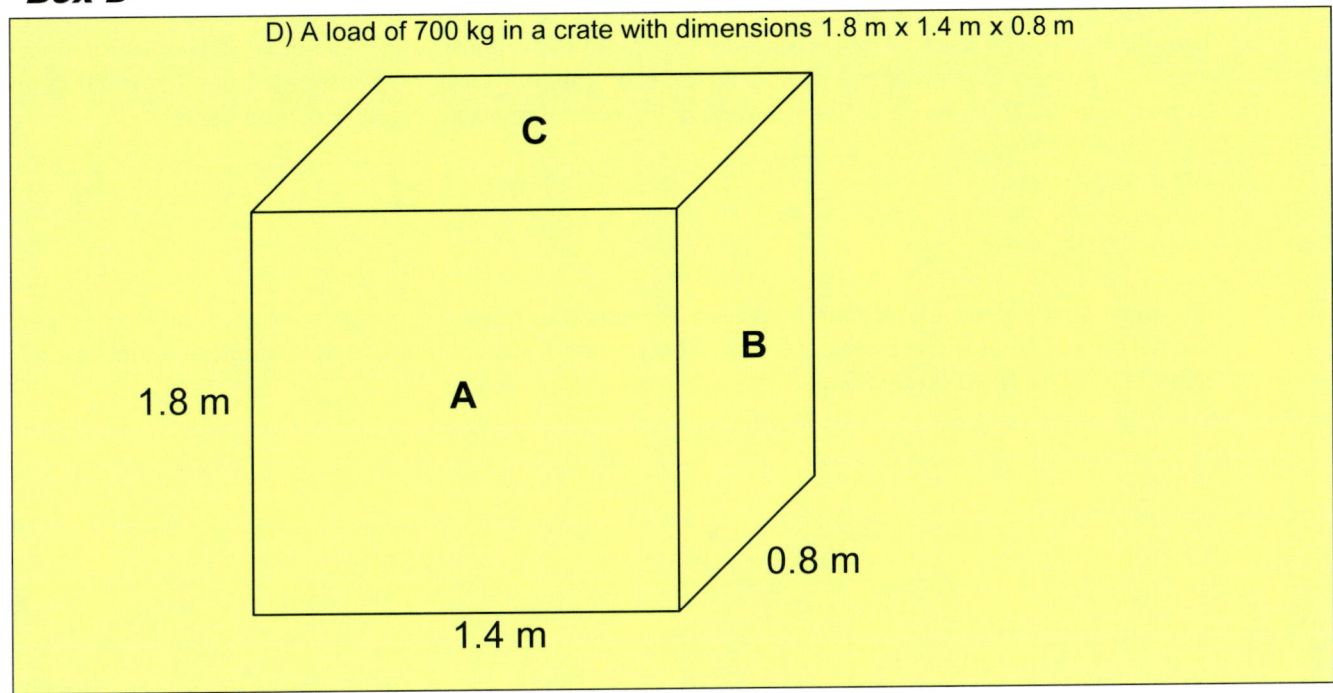

D) A load of 700 kg in a crate with dimensions 1.8 m x 1.4 m x 0.8 m

Side		Area		Distribution Load
Side A =	1.8 x 1.4	=	2.52 m^2	278 kg / m^2
Side B =	1.8 x 0.8	=	1.44 m^2	486 kg / m^2
Side C =	1.4 x 0.8	=	1.12 m^2	625 kg / m^2

With reference to the distribution load, the maximum is 300 kg / m^2. Only one of the values is below 300 kg / m^2 so now move onto calculating the running load to see if that one side is safe enough to be loaded onto the aircraft.

Mass ÷ Length			Running Load
= 700	÷	1.8	388 kg / m
= 700	÷	1.4	500 kg / m
= 700	÷	0.8	875 kg / m

With reference to the running load, the maximum is 350 kg / m. All of the above values are above 350 kg / m so the package will exceed the maximum load on the aircraft runners.

Therefore in conclusion, answer A with a box weighing 400 kg with dimensions of 1.2 m x 1.2 m x 1.2 m is the only package that may be placed onto the aircraft without exceeding the distribution or running loads.

EASA STUDY GUIDES

MASS & BALANCE

Mass and Balance Self Assessment Test 06

1. The maximum floor loading for a cargo compartment in an aeroplane is given as 750 kg per square metre. A package with a mass of 600 kg is to be loaded. Assuming the pallet base is entirely in contact with the floor, which of the following is the minimum size pallet that can be used?
A) 40 cm by 200 cm
B) 30 cm by 300 cm
C) 30 cm by 200 cm
D) 40 cm by 300 cm

2. The maximum intensity floor loading for an aeroplane is given in the Flight Manual as 650 kg per square metre. What is the maximum mass of a package, which can be safely supported, on a pallet with dimensions of 80 cm by 80 cm?
A) 416.0 kg
B) 1015.6 kg
C) 41.6 kg
D) 101.6 kg

EASA STUDY GUIDES

MASS & BALANCE

Mass and Balance Self Assessment Test 06 ANSWERS

1	A
2	A

CHAPTER 7
Loading a Single-Engine Piston Aeroplane

7.1 Introduction

This chapter is devoted to the examination of the loading of a light aeroplane. The aeroplane used is a generic single engine piston aircraft (SEP1) details of which are contained in the JAR FCL EXAMINATIONS MASS & BALANCE MANUAL (CAP 696) (Data sheets for use in European Professional Pilot"s Licence Examinations).

It should be noted that the first four pages of CAP 696 are devoted to general notes, which include aircraft descriptions, definitions and some conversion factors.

The landing gear position does not significantly affect CG position in this sample SEP1 aeroplane.

7.1.1 Example 1

C.G. arm = (moment x 100) / Mass

Page 9 (*Figure 2.5*) of CAP 696 is the C.G. envelope against which calculated C.G. arms should be checked to ensure C.G. is within limits. The diagram allows an option avoiding the calculation: HORIZONTAL Mass lines may be intersected with SLOPING (top left to bottom right) lines of Moment x 100 to derive C.G. arm.

Example 1 of LOADING MANIFEST for aircraft SEP1
The following are to be carried on a flight in aeroplane SEP1:
Pilot (actual mass, including equipment): 200 lbs.
2 passengers in third and fourth seats (actual total mass 380 lbs.)
Passenger baggage in zone B (actual mass 55 lbs.)
200 lbs. of freight in baggage zone C
50 gallons of fuel (at start up)

Complete the LOADING MANIFEST for this flight and ensure C.G. is within limits
Solution: see following pages

EASA STUDY GUIDES

MASS & BALANCE

ITEM	MASS	ARM (IN)	MOMENT x 100
1. BASIC EMPTY CONDITION	2415	77.70	1876.46
2. FRONT SEAT OCCUPANTS	200	79.00	158.00
3. THIRD & FOURTH SEAT PAX	380.00	117.00	444.60
4. BAGGAGE ZONE 'A'	NIL	108.00	NIL
5. FIFTH AND SIXTH SEAT PAX	NIL	152.00	NIL
6. BAGGAGE ZONE 'B'	55	150.00	82.50
7. BAGGAGE ZONE 'C'	200.00	180.00	360.00
SUB-TOTAL = ZERO FUEL MASS	**3250**	**89.90**	**2921.56**
8. FUEL LOADING	300	75.00	225.00
SUB-TOTAL = RAMP MASS	**3550**	**88.60**	**3146.56**
9. SUBTRACT FUEL FROM START-UP TAXI & RUN UP	13.00	0.769	10.00
SUB-TOTAL = TAKE OFF MASS	**3537**	**88.70**	**3136.56**
10. TRIP FUEL (SUBTRACT)	-210.00	75.00	-157.50
SUB TOTAL = LANDING MASS	**3327**	**89.50**	**2979.06**

Figure 0.1 SEP1 Loading Manifest

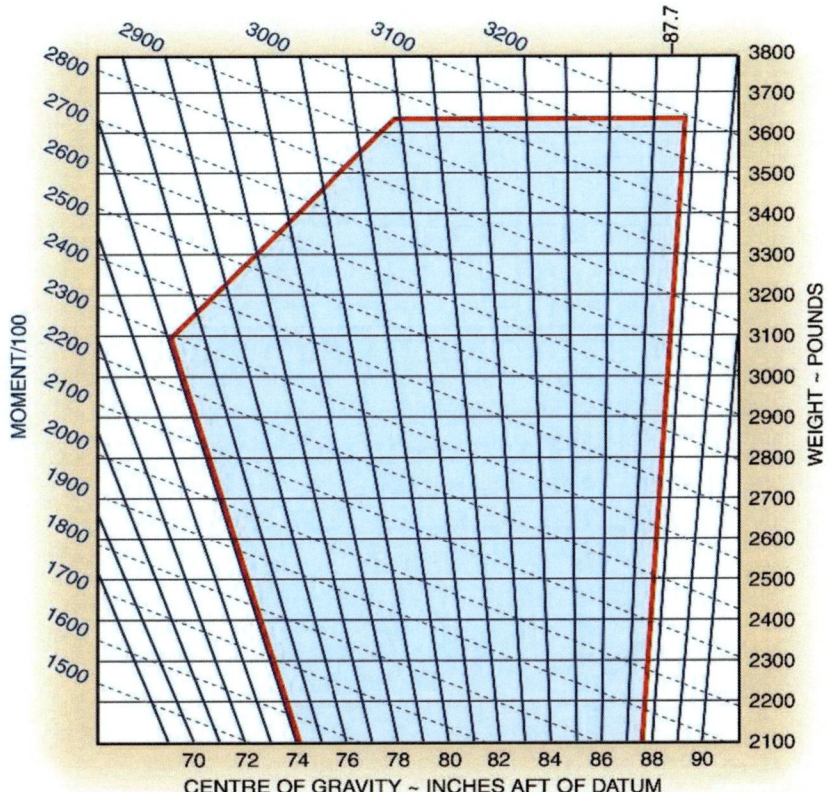

Figure 0.2 CG Envelope

The C.G. has been calculated for each sub-total and checked against the envelope at Fig 2.5 in the loading manual.

```
At ZFM:       2921.56 x 100 / 3250 = 89.9 inches:  OUT OF LIMITS
At Ramp Mass  3146.56 x 100 / 3550 = 88.6 inches   OUT OF LIMITS
At TOM        3136.56 x 100 / 3537 = 88.7 inches   OUT OF LIMITS
At LM         2979.06 x 100 / 3327 = 89.5 inches   OUT OF LIMITS
```

7.1.2 Example 2

On inspection it is apparent that the probable cause of the out of limits C.G. situation is the amount of freight in baggage zone C.

It is decided to switch freight to zone B and also to seat the heavier of the 2 passengers (200 lbs) in the empty front seat, next to the pilot. The LOADING MANIFEST must now be revised.

ITEM	MASS	ARM (IN)	MOMENT x 100
1. BASIC EMPTY CONDITION	2415	77.70	1876.46
2. FRONT SEAT OCCUPANTS	400.00	79.00	316.00
3. THIRD & FOURTH SEAT PAX	180.00	117.00	210.60
4. BAGGAGE ZONE 'A'	NIL	108.00	NIL
5. FIFTH AND SIXTH SEAT PAX	NIL	152.00	NIL
6. BAGGAGE ZONE 'B'	255	150.00	382.50
7. BAGGAGE ZONE 'C'		180.00	
SUB-TOTAL = ZERO FUEL MASS	**3250**	**85.70**	**2785.56**
8. FUEL LOADING	300	75.00	225.00
SUB-TOTAL = RAMP MASS	**3550**	**84.80**	**3010.56**
9. SUBTRACT FUEL FROM START-UP TAXI & RUN UP	-13.00		-10.00
SUB-TOTAL = TAKE OFF MASS	**3537**	**84.80**	**3000.56**
10. TRIP FUEL (SUBTRACT)	210.00	75.00	157.50
SUB TOTAL = LANDING MASS	**3327**	**85.50**	**2843.06**

Figure 7.3 Revised loading manifest example 2

The CG has again been calculated for each sub-total and checked against the envelope (*in Fig 2.5 in the data sheet.*)

At ZFM: 2785.56 x 100 / 3250 = 85.7 inches: WITHIN LIMITS
At Ramp Mass 3010.56 x 100 / 3550 = 84.8 inches WITHIN LIMITS
At TOM   3000.56 x 100 / 3537 = 84.8 inches WITHIN LIMITS
At LM   2843.06 x 100 / 3327 = 85.5 inches WITHIN LIMITS

CHAPTER 8
Loading a Light Twin-Engine Piston Aeroplane

8.1 Introduction

This chapter is devoted to the examination of the loading of a light twin-engined aeroplane. The aeroplane used is a generic multi engine piston aircraft (MEP1) details of which are contained in the JAR FCL EXAMINATIONS MASS & BALANCE MANUAL (CAP 696) (Data sheets for use in European Professional Pilot's Licence Examinations). The sample aeroplane is designated MEP1. The details appear in the CIVIL AVIATION AUTHORITY JAR FCL EXAMINATIONS MASS & BALANCE MANUAL:

The manual gives a general description about the aircraft such as:
- The reference datum is not at the nose of the aeroplane
- C.G. limits are given: the aft limit is fixed, the forward limit varies with mass
- Limitations are given for MTOM, MLM and MZFM
- The BEM and its arm are given
- Landing gear position does not significantly affect the C.G.
- The floor structural loading limit is given

8.1.1 Example 1

The following are to be carried over a route requiring 98 US gallons of fuel (Including 38 US gallons to cover reserves and fuel allowance for start-up, taxi and run-up):
- 1 pilot: 210 lb
- 3 passengers: 200 lb, 185 lb and 170 lb
- Passenger baggage: 125 lb total
- Freight: 50 lb

Examining weight restraints leads to the following loading plan:
- 200 lb for a front seat passenger
- total mass of 355 lb to occupy the centre seats
- 1 case (45 lb) and freight (50 lb) to be stowed in baggage zone 1
- 2 cases (80 lbs) will be stowed in baggage zone 3
- The Loading Manifest is now completed and the C.G. derived for each of: Zero Fuel Mass; Ramp Mass; Take-off Mass; Landing Mass

EASA STUDY GUIDES

MASS & BALANCE

ITEM	MASS (lbs)	ARM Aft of Datum (inches)	MOMENT (inches/lbs)
Basic Empty Mass	3210	88.50	284085.00
Pilot and Front Passenger	410.00	85.50	35055.00
Passenger (centre seats) or baggage zone 2 (360 lb max)	355.00	118.50	42067.50
Passenger (centre seats) or baggage zone 3 (400 lb max)	80.00	157.60	12608.00
Baggage zone 1	95.00	22.50	2137.50
Baggage zone 4		178.70	
Zero Fuel Mass (4470 lb max-std)	4150	90.59	375953.00
Fuel (123 Gal. Max)	588.00	93.60	55036.80
Ramp Mass (4773 lb Max)	4738	90.96	430989.80
Fuel allowance from start-up, taxi, run-up	-24.00	93.60	-2246.40
Take-off mass (4750 lb Max)	4714	90.95	428743.40
Minus Estimated fuel burn-off	-360	93.60	-33696.00
Landing Mass (4513 lb Max)	4354	90.73	395047.40

Figure 8.1 Loading Manifest MEP1

Maximum mass values given in this table are for structural limits only

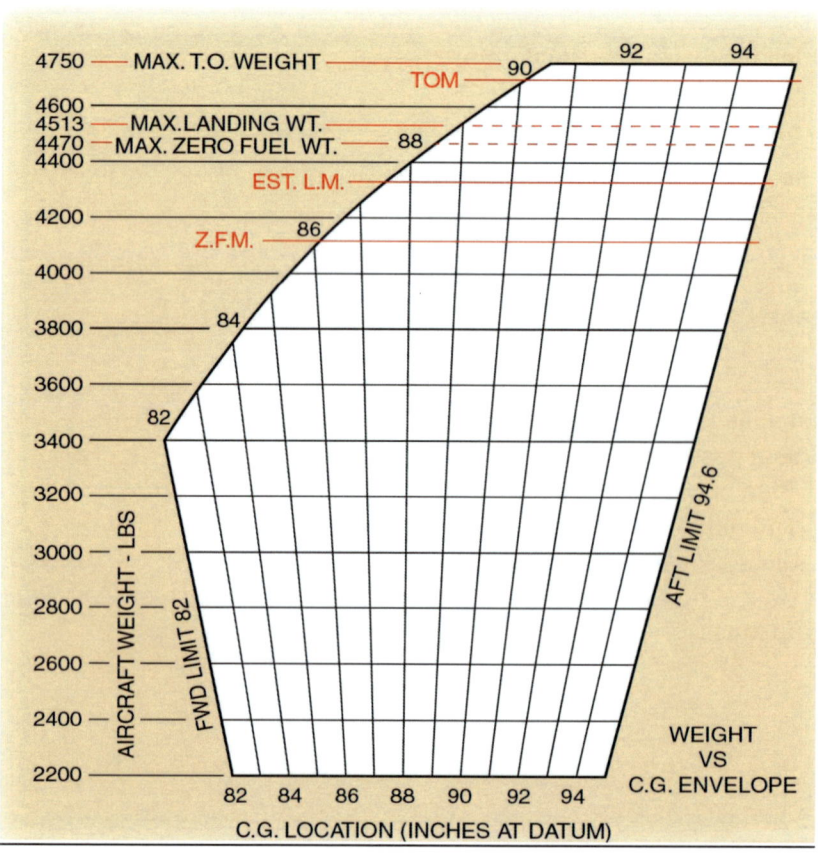

Figure 8.2 CG. envelope for example 1

CHAPTER 9
Loading a Transport Aeroplane

9.1 Introduction

The third of the generic aeroplanes given in the CAA JAR FCL Examinations Mass & Balance Manual is a medium range twin jet, (MRJT 1) certified under FAR / JAR-25 in performance Class A.

This section of the CAP 696 is utilised in the ATPL examination but is not required for CPL students.

The first page of the MRJT CAP696 aircraft defines the balance arms in inches and shows where the reference datum is on the aircraft. The datum point is 540 inches forward of the front spar.

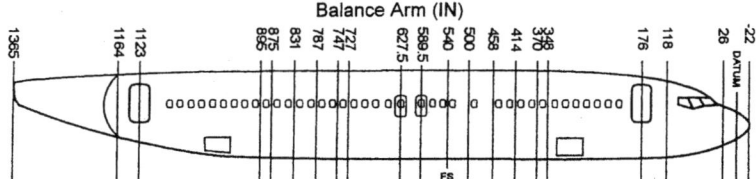

Figure 4.1 Locations Diagram

Figure 4-.2 TABLE TO CONVERT BODY STATION TO BALANCE ARM

BODY STATION	CONVERSION	BALANCE ARM - IN
130 to 500	B.S. – 152 IN	-22 to 348
500A	348 + 22 IN	370
500B	348 + 44 IN	392
500C	348 + 66 IN	414
500D	348 + 88 IN	436
500E	348 +110 IN	458
500F	348 +132 IN	480
500G	348 +152 IN	500
540 to 727	B.S. + 0 IN	540 to 727
727A	727 + 20 IN	747
727B	727 + 40 IN	767
727C	727 + 60 IN	787
727D	727 + 82 IN	809
727E	727 +104 IN	831
727F	727 +126 IN	853
727G	727 +148 IN	875
747 to 1217	B.S. +148 IN	895 to 1365

2.1 Datum point   540 inches forward of front spar (FS)

2.2 Landing Gear Retraction/extension — negligible effect from operation of landing gear

1.3 Flap Retraction

Figure 4.3   Effect of flap retraction

From	To	Moment Change (Kg – inches x 1000)
5	0	-11
15	0	-14
30	0	-15
40	0	-16

The next section of the MRJT1 explains what happens to the centre of gravity (CG) with reference to landing gear retraction and extension. The effect of flap retraction is also explained and shows for example that if the flap setting is change from 30 to 0 then the moment change is –15000. If there is a minus figure then this means that the CG has moved forward.

The above section of the MRJT1 shows a graph to illustrate what happens to the % MAC with varying

1.4 Take-off Horizontal Stabiliser Trim Setting

Figure 4.4   Graph of trim units for C.G. position

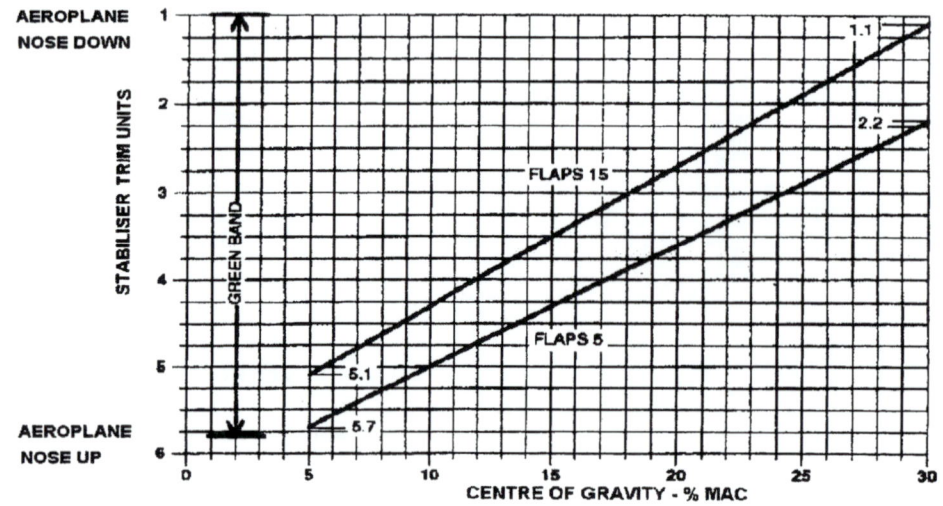

stabiliser trim units.

> Example:
>
> Flap setting 15, stabiliser trim setting is 3, what is the % MAC?
>
> Answer: **18% MAC**

EASA STUDY GUIDES

MASS & BALANCE

2.5 Mean Aerodynamic Chord	134.5 inches
Leading edge 625.6 inches aft of datum

3. MASS AND BALANCE LIMITATIONS

3.1 Mass Limits

Maximum Structural Taxi Mass	63060
Maximum Structural Take-off Mass	62800
Maximum Structural Landing Mass	54900
Maximum Structural Zero Fuel Mass	51300

MASS & BALANCE   21

Some questions in the examination provides very basic information with reference to mean aerodynamic chord but you need to know where to find additional information to help you attain an accurate answer. This information may also be found on page 21 of CAP 696 (MRJT).

The maximum masses are also given and these need to be used in the load and trim sheet when calculating traffic load.

4. FUEL

4.1

Figure 4.5   Fuel Tank Location and Maximum Volume

	BA (full tanks)	Volume (US Gallons)	Mass (Kg)
Left Wing Main Tank 1	650.7	1499	4542
Right Wing Main Tank 2	650.7	1499	4542
Centre Tank	600.4	2313	7008
Max. Total Fuel (assumes 3.03 Kg/US Gall.)	628.8	5311	16092

Caution – If centre tank contains more than 450 Kg the wing tanks **must** be full.

4.2

Figure 4.6   Unusable Fuel Quantities

Location	Volume (US Galls)	Mass (Kg)	BA
Wing Tank 1	4.6	14.0	599.0
Wing Tank 2	4.6	14.0	599.0
Centre Tank	7.9	24.0	600.9

The following section of MRJT aircraft on page 24 defines how much usable and unusable fuel is found in each one of the three tanks on the aircraft, as well as showing you the balance arm for each tank if a CG calculation is required.

5. PASSENGERS (PAX) AND PERSONNEL

5.1 Maximum Passenger Load 141
    Club/Business 33
    Economy 108

5.2 Passenger Distribution

Figure 4.7 shows the balance arms (in inches) for the distribution of passengers. If the pax load is low, zones B, C and D are the preferred seating areas.

Figure 4.7   BALANCE ARMS (IN)

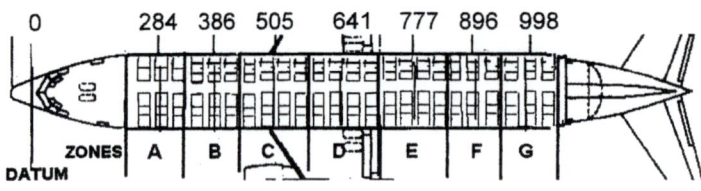

Figure 4.8   Table of pax. Zones /Balance Arms

ZONE	NO. PAX	B.A.
A	15	284
B	18	386
C	24	505
D	24	641
E	24	777
F	18	896
G	18	998

5.3 Passenger Mass

Unless otherwise stated passenger mass is assumed to be 84 Kg. (this includes a 6 Kg. allowance for hand baggage)

5.4 Passenger Baggage

Unless otherwise stated a baggage allowance of 13 Kg may be made per passenger.

5.5 Personnel

Standard Crewing

	No.	BA	Standard Mass (Kg) each
Flight Deck	2	78.0	90
Cabin Staff Forward	2	162.0	90
Cabin Staff Aft	1	1107.0	90

This following section shows the number of passengers per zone as well as the standard masses for passengers and their baggage.

EASA STUDY GUIDES

MASS & BALANCE

FORWARD CARGO COMPARTMENT

BA – IN	228	286	343	500
MAXIMUM COMPARTMENT RUNNING LOAD (Kg. per IN.)		13.15	8.47	13.12
MAXIMUM DISTRIBUTION LOAD INTENSITY (Kg. per Ft.^{2})			68	
MAXIMUM COMPARTMENT LOAD (Kg)		762	483	2059
COMPARTMENT CENTROID (BA – IN)		257	314.5	421.5
MAXIMUM TOTAL LOAD (Kg.)			3305	
FWD HOLD CENTROID (BA – IN)			367.9	
FWD HOLD VOLUME (CU. Ft.)			607	

AFT CARGO COMPARTMENT

BA – IN	731	940	997	1096
MAXIMUM COMPARTMENT RUNNING LOAD (Kg. per IN)		14.65	7.26	7.18
MAXIMUM DISTRIBUTION LOAD INTENSITY (Kg. per Ft.^{2})			68	
MAXIMUM COMPARTMENT LOAD (Kg)		3062	414	711
COMPARTMENT CENTROID (BA – IN)		835.5	968.5	1046.5
MAXIMUM TOTAL LOAD (Kg.)			4187	
FWD HOLD CENTROID (BA – IN)			884.5	
FWD HOLD VOLUME (CU. Ft.)			766	

This next section from the MRJT1 CAP 696 represents the maximum loading in each one of the aircrafts loading bays.
Be careful to read the units before you jump to any conclusions.

> **Example 1:**
>
> Referring to the loading manual for the transport aeroplane, the maximum running load for the aft section of the forward lower deck cargo compartment is:
>   7.18 kg per inch
>   13.12 lbs per inch
>   13.12 kg per inch
>   14.65 kg per inch

Find out what is asked for, i.e. the maximum compartment running load, and then find out if it is the aft cargo hold or the forward cargo hold. In mass and balance calculations aft is to the right so therefore the aft limit is the one on the far right.

> **Answer: 13.12 kg per inch**

CRANFIELD AVIATION TRAINING SCHOOL LTD. PART-FCL ATO N° 276
CATS INNOVATION CENTRE, LUTON, Bedfordshire LU2 8DL U.K.

www.catsaviation.com

EASA STUDY GUIDES

MASS & BALANCE

9.1.1 Use of Passenger Mass, Crew Mass Data

This data is presented in a fairly self-evident fashion. The information regarding 'Standard Mass' values for passengers and their baggage is NOT identical to JAR-OPS Section J data. So be sure to read any question carefully.

Standard Mass values for crew include an allowance for personal baggage.

9.1.1.1 Example 1

> Determine the C.G. for the aeroplane from the loading manifest. Ensure that the C.G. remains within the envelope throughout the flight.

ITEM	MASS (kg)	Balance Arm (inches)	MOMENT (kg-inch / 1000)	CG % MAC
DOM	34500	649.00	22390.5	-
2. PAX ZONE A	840.00	284.00	238.60	-
3. PAX ZONE B	1512	386.00	583.60	-
4. PAX ZONE C	2016	505.00	1018.10	-
5. PAX ZONE D	2016	641.00	1292.30	-
6. PAX ZONE E	2016	777.00	1566.40	-
7. PAX ZONE F	1512	896.00	1354.80	-
8. PAX ZONE G	1092	998.00	1089.80	-
9. CARGO HOLD 1	650.00	367.90	239.10	-
10. CARGO HOLD 4	2120	884.90	1875.10	-
11. ADDITIONAL ITEMS	NIL	NIL	NIL	-
ZERO FUEL MASS	**48274**	**655.60**	**31648.3**	**22.30**
12. FUEL TANKS 1 & 2	9084	650.70	5911	-
13. CENTRE TANK	4916	600.40	2951.60	-
TAXI MASS	**62274**	**650.50**	**40510.9**	**18.50**
LESS TAXI FUEL	-260.0	600.40	-156.10	-
TAKE OFF MASS	**62014**	**650.70**	**40354.8**	**18.70**
LESS FLIGHT FUEL	4844 4656 (TOTAL=9500)	650.7 600.4	-3152 -2795.5	-
EST. LANDING MASS	**52514**	**655.20**	**34407.3**	**22.53**

Figure 9.1 MRJT1 Loading Manifest

Max Permissible Aeroplane Mass Values:

> TAXI MASS   - 63060 kg
> ZERO FUEL MASS   - 51300 kg
> TAKE OFF MASS   - 62800 kg
> LANDING MASS   - 54900 kg

> Centre Tank has 4916 kg at start-up but uses 260 kg to taxi to the runway. It therefore has 4656 kg when lined up on the runway

When each of ZFM, TOM and Est. LM is checked with its C.G. % MAC at Figure 4.11 of CAP 696 all are found to be in limits.

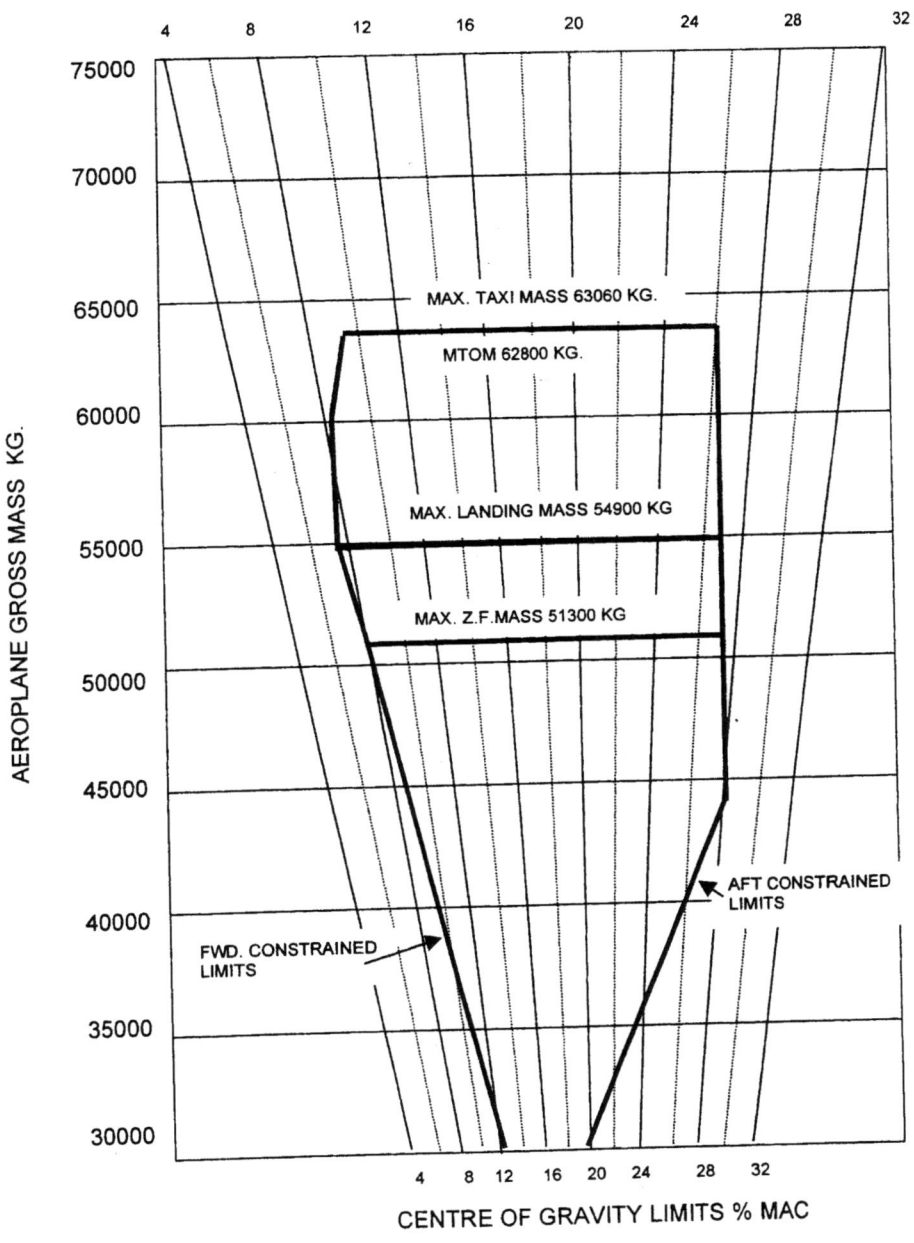

Figure 9.2 CG envelope (MRJT1)

EASA STUDY GUIDES

MASS & BALANCE

Mass and Balance Self Assessment Test 09

1. (For this question use the Loading Manual MRJT 1 Figure 4.11)
   At the maximum landing mass the range of safe CG positions, as determined from the appropriate graph in the loading manual, is:
   A) Forward limit 8.0% MAC aft limit 27.2% MAC
   B) Forward limit 8.6% MAC aft limit 27.0% MAC
   C) Forward limit 8.0% MAC aft limit 26.8% MAC
   D) Forward limit 7.4% MAC aft limit 27.0% MAC

2. (For this question use the Loading Manual MRJT 1 Figure 4.9)
   For the transport aeroplane the moment (balance) arm (B.A.) for the forward hold centroid is:
   A) 314.5 inches
   B) 421.5 inches
   C) 367.9 inches
   D) 257 inches

3. (For this question use the Loading Manual MRJT 1 Figure 4.9)
   Referring to the loading manual for the transport aeroplane, the maximum running load for the aft section of the forward lower deck cargo compartment is:
   A) 7.18 kg per inch.
   B) 13.12 kg per inch.
   C) 13.15 kg per inch.
   D) 14.65 kg per inch.

4. (For this question use the Loading Manual MRJT 1 Figure 4.9)
   From the loading manual for the jet transport aeroplane, the maximum floor loading intensity for the aft cargo compartment is :
   A) 68 kg per square foot
   B) 150 kg per square foot
   C) 68 Lbs per square foot
   D) 68 kg per square metre

5. (For this question use the Loading Manual MRJT 1 Figure 4.9)
   From the Loading Manual for the transport aeroplane, the maximum load that can be carried in that section of the aft cargo compartment which has a balance arm centroid at :
   A) 421.5 inches is 4541 kg
   B) 421.5 inches is 2059 lb
   C) 835.5 inches is 3062 kg
   D) 835.5 inches is 6752 kg

EASA STUDY GUIDES

MASS & BALANCE

Mass and Balance Self Assessment Test 09 ANSWERS

1	D
2	C
3	B
4	A
5	C